Painting Faux
Stained Glass

Painting Faux
Stained Glass

Sterling Publishing Co., Inc. New York
A Sterling / Chapelle Book

Chapelle, Ltd.:
- Owner: Jo Packham
- Editor: Laura Best

- Staff: Areta Bingham, Kass Burchett, Marilyn Goff, Holly Hollingsworth,
            Susan Jorgensen, Kimberly Maw, Barbara Milburn, Linda Orton,
            Karmen Quinney, Cindy Stoeckl, Kim Taylor, Sara Toliver, Kristi Torsak

Plaid Enterprises:
- Editor: Mickey Baskett

- Staff: Sylvia Carroll, Jeff Herr, Laney McClure, Susan Mickey, Dianne Miller,
            Jerry Mucklow, Phyllis Mueller, Rachel Watkins, Suzanne Yoder
- Artists: Kim Ballor, Laura Brunson, Jan Cumber, Wendy Dyer, Jacque Hennington,
            Nance Kueneman, Sue Leonard, Julie Schreiner, Carol Smith, Kirsten Werner

If you have any questions or comments, please contact:
Chapelle, Ltd., Inc., P.O. Box 9252, Ogden, UT 84409
(801) 621-2777 • (801) 621-2788 Fax
chapelle@chapelleltd.com • www.chapelleltd.com

Library of Congress Cataloging-in-Publication Data

10 9 8 7 6 5 4 3 2 1

Published by Sterling Publishing Company, Inc.
387 Park Avenue South, New York, NY 10016
©2001 by Plaid Enterprises
Distributed in Canada by Sterling Publishing
c/o Canadian Manda Group, One Atlantic Avenue, Suite 105
Toronto, Ontario, Canada M6K 3E7
Distributed in Great Britain and Europe by Cassell PLC
Wellington House, 125 Strand, London WCR2 OBB, England
Distributed in Australia by Capricorn Link (Australia) Pty Ltd.
P.O. Box 704, Windsor, NSW 2756, Australia
Printed in China
All Rights Reserved

Sterling ISBN 0-8069-2961-8

Introduction

Enjoy the centuries-old art form of stained-glass windows made easy and accessible with the techniques explained in this book. Delight in the beauty of stained-glass windows reflecting colorful or refracted light. This craft has been made easy with step-by-step instructions, patterns for designs, and easy to find supplies. You can create the look of authentic stained glass without the expense or skill.

Windows in your home can become works of art. Also included with the stunning array of windows are small screens to sit on a window ledge, suncatchers to hang in windows, and glass panels for doors.

The method used to create these windows is simple and fun. These projects are all made with Glass Art Paint that can be squeezed from the bottle onto the window's surface. You will find in this book instructions for a number of ways to decorate your windows with this effortless craft.

Table of

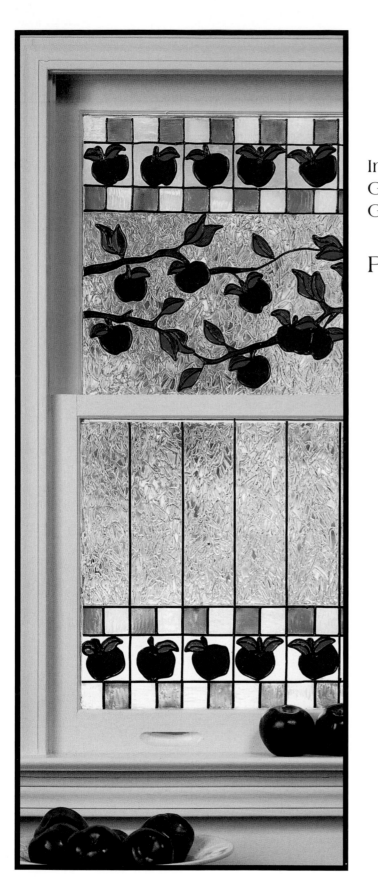

Contents

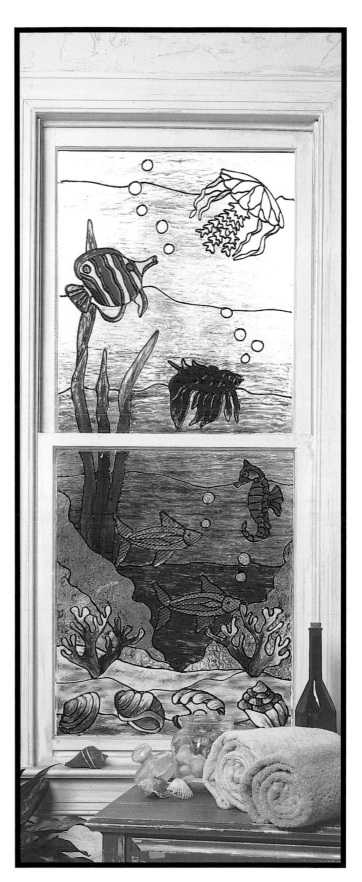

General Supplies

PAINT

Translucent textured Glass Art Paint is a special water-based paint that dries to a transparent, textured finish, simulating the look of custom stained glass. It can be applied to glass or plastic surfaces. Available in many beautiful colors, Glass Art Paint comes in a plastic squeeze bottle with an applicator tip, so it is easy to apply paint directly to surfaces.

Also available in the Glass Art Paint selection are iridescent colors. Iridescent colors appear to be one color when they reflect light at night, and another when daylight shines through the design. They can be used alone or mixed with other paints to add a sheen of color. Several colors marbleized with White Pearl or Crystal Clear produce a soft mother-of-pearl look.

DO NOT apply Glass Art Paint to surfaces when temperatures are less than 45° F or above 90° F. Extremes in temperature during the application and curing process can cause cracking and distortion.

DO NOT use outdoors or in environments that are not temperature controlled. Also avoid using surfaces that are in frequent contact with water or heavy condensation.

DO NOT shake paint bottles causing paints to separate.

SPECIAL EFFECTS MEDIUMS

There are several paint products designed to give special textures and effects.

Crackle Medium—can create the look of textured, cracked glass. Apply with a paintbrush over dried paint.

Etching Medium—can create the look or feel of etched glass. Apply with a sponge or paintbrush to the glass surface (not over dried paint).

Matte Medium—can create the look of authentic, aged stained glass. Apply with a paintbrush, over dried paint.

LEADING

Leading is used to separate paint colors and add design to glass. Leading can be purchased in premade strips or, using liquid leading and leading blanks, can be made at home.

Premade Leading Strips—can be purchased already formed into lines that peel off and stick to windows.

Liquid Leading—when dry, forms leading strips. To use, squeeze leading onto a leading blank, outlining an entire design or making leading strips to use later. Liquid leading cannot be applied to a vertical surface. Let leading dry before applying to window. The strips are bendable and can follow curves and design lines. Liquid leading is available in black, gold glitter, gold metallic, silver glitter, and silver metallic.

Leading Blanks—are 8" x 10" plastic sheets used as a surface to create leading lines. Designs can be created on blanks, then removed and applied to windows. The texture of these blanks makes it easy to remove strips or entire painted designs from the surface.

Other Supplies:

Black Transfer Paper—for transferring designs onto glass surfaces.

Craft Knife—for trimming leading.

Craft Stick & Disposable Foam Container—for mixing paint colors together to create a new color.

Glass Cleaner—for cleaning surfaces before applying leading.

Paper Towels—for drying glass and wiping bottle tips and fingers.

Pencil—for tracing patterns onto tracing paper.

Scissors—for trimming leading and cutting out traced patterns.

Tool Set—consisting of a nutpick for combing paint, a multipurpose tool for scooping and combing paint, a leading trimmer for cutting leading, and a palette knife for spreading paint.

Toothpicks—for combing out bubbles in paint.

Tracing Paper—for tracing patterns and motifs from the book.

Yardstick or Ruler—for measuring and marking.

General Instructions

WINDOW PREPARATION

1. Protect work surface with paper towels.

2. Clean glass surface with glass cleaner, or wash with soap and water. Let dry.

3. Measure window or surface and adjust design measurements.

4. Draw or choose pattern to fit window.

5. Practice applying leading strips on surface. Get the feel of applying paints. Remember that you are working on glass. Do not use excessive pressure when applying or removing materials.

APPLICATION TECHNIQUES

The application techniques shown in this book offer a variety of ways to create stained-glass designs. The three most popular techniques are the Vertical Technique, the Modular Technique, and the Horizontal Technique. Each technique, while similar, has its own merits.

The Horizontal Technique is used if the surface can be placed horizontally for working. This allows the leading and painting to be done directly on the project and on a flat surface.

The Modular Technique is an alternate way to create designs for vertical surfaces. This technique is more commonly used on smaller motifs or when the surface cannot be laid horizontally. The design motifs are leaded, painted, and cured on a leading blank surface. After the design motif is dry, it is peeled up and placed on the window.

The Vertical Technique is for working on windows that are already in place and cannot be removed or placed on a work surface.

WORKING WITH PATTERNS

Patterns are supplied for each project. When a design is symmetrical, often only half of the design is presented. Flip the design to create a mirror image. Trace designs on tracing paper to keep the book intact. Place traced pattern behind or under glass surface or transfer onto glass with black transfer paper.

Paint colors are indicated on each color guide by number. These numbers represent the colors given in the supplies list with each project. If two or more colors are indicated with a / sign, loosely blend or swirl colors together within the section. If a number appears within a circle, marbleize the colors within that section. Apply background color first, then apply dots of color indicated in the circles. Use applicator tip or toothpick to swirl colors together.

Adjusting Patterns

Determine how many repetitions of the pattern are necessary for the project. Compare the window size to the pattern. To adjust the pattern size, either add/remove borders, or enlarge/reduce pattern using a photocopy machine.

Use the following formulas to adjust the size of patterns in this book:

To enlarge a pattern:
$$\frac{\text{desired size} \div \text{size of pattern}}{\text{\% of enlargement}}$$

To reduce a pattern:
$$\frac{\text{desired size} \div \text{size of pattern}}{\text{\% of reduction}}$$

EXAMPLE:
$$\frac{12" \text{ (desired size)} \div 6" \text{ (current size)}}{2.00}$$
(200% enlargement)

EXAMPLE:
$$\frac{4" \text{ (desired size)} \div 6" \text{ (current size)}}{.66}$$
(66% reduction)

Making Leading Strips

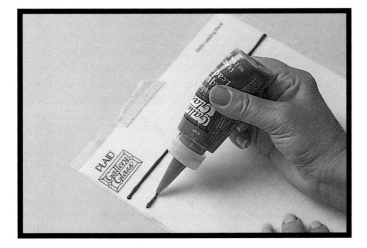

Since liquid leading cannot be applied directly to a vertical surface, leading strips need to be prepared and dried before applying to the surface. Unscrew the liquid leading bottle cap and remove the seal. Before replacing the top, use a paper clip or nutpick to make a hole in the tip. Be certain hole is large enough for leading to flow freely. Do not cut tip off yet. Replace cap. Hold the bottle upside down and tap firmly on a hard surface to force leading into tip. Remove cap and cut tip when ready to use.

Hold inverted bottle securely. Do not rest elbow on work surface—it will inhibit movement. Squeeze lines of leading (⅛"–³⁄₁₆" diameter) on a leading blank, using lines as guides.

Leading strips can be made on purchased leading blanks. For ease in making straight lines, place a piece of lined notebook paper under the blank.

To make leading blanks, place lined notebook paper on a piece of cardboard and cover with nonclinging plastic wrap. Do not use hard plastics that resemble glass because the liquid leading and paint will adhere permanently to such surfaces.

Let leading cure thoroughly (at least 72 hours) until the strips peel up cleanly.

Tips for Working with Leading Strips
- Mistakes in leading can be corrected by scoring it with a craft knife and peeling it away, then reapplying new leading.

- Messy lines can be corrected with practice and by coordinating the pressure on the bottle with the forward movement of the bottle. Practice on notebook paper to master the rhythm.

- Beginning bumps can be eliminated by anchoring the leading to the glass so leading will not curl around the tip and create the bumps before beginning the line.

- Ending bumps can be avoided by stopping the squeeze before reaching the end of the line and bring tip down, allowing the line to end.

- Trim blotches from leading strips with a craft knife before applying to glass surface.

- Avoid pulling or stretching strips.

- Avoid handling strips more than necessary.

- Piece strips by placing them end to end. Do not overlap strips. When lines intersect, trim them neatly with a craft knife.

- Touch up gaps by squeezing a small amount of liquid leading on them. Let joints dry thoroughly before applying background.

- If a wider line is desired, apply two strips side by side and fill the gap with liquid leading.

- To emulate the look of soldered joints, add small blobs of liquid leading to the intersecting lines. When dry, rub silver gilding on leading for a realistic look.

Making Flat or Fine Leading Lines

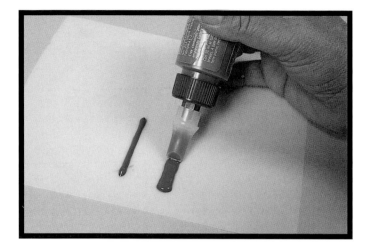

Flat leading creates a true glass-art look for cabinet doors and sidelights. With flat leading, ends can be overlapped without bulk. Miter corners with a craft knife, and control the width of your leading. Use a flat leading tip that is sold separately where glass-art supplies are found.

Thin leading can be used for adding details or intricate designs or even write words. Fine-line leading tips can be purchased or you can make your own.

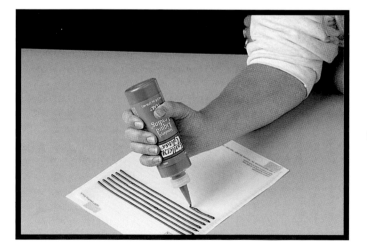

To make your own fine-line leading tip, use the following steps:

1. Make a hole in the tip, following manufacturer's instructions. Squeeze gently to dispense. Cut a 3½" strip of ¾"-wide cellophane tape. Place left edge of tape along the center of the tip. Press tape to spout as you rotate the bottle, securing the first turn of the tape and making a leak-proof seal.

2. As you turn the bottle, the tape will form a cone. Press tape firmly to the tip to prevent puckering. Continue turning the bottle, adhering tape to previous layers.

3. The tape will reverse directions when the fine-line tip is formed. Continue to turn bottle, allowing tape to wind down.

Press any extra tape over the side of the cap for easy removal later. To make a thicker line of leading, snip cone ⅛".

Using Premade Leading Strips

1 Simply peel away a strip of premade leading.

3 Where leading lines connect to one another, use liquid leading to fill gaps or "solder" the joints.

2 Position premade leading strip on glass surface, following pattern lines. Although strips may be curved to fit lines, avoid stretching. Avoid handling strips more than necessary or they may not adhere properly.

If a pattern line is longer than the strip, piece strips together end to end. Intersecting and meeting lines should be trimmed so they connect without overlapping.

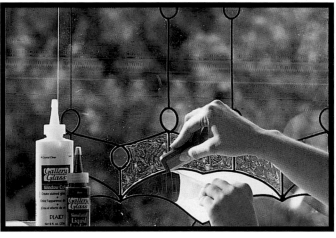

4 If paint needs to be removed or changed, the leading will remain in place.

Using the Horizontal Technique

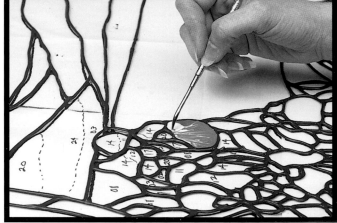

1 Place pattern under glass, Plexiglas®, or styrene panel. Apply leading evenly. It may help to raise the tip 1" above the work surface to allow leading to drape evenly along pattern lines. Let leading dry at least eight hours. When dry, remove unwanted leading and trim with small scissors.

3 To create a smooth texture and minimize bubbles, comb vigorously back and forth through paint with nutpick. Arrows on patterns indicate the direction to comb.

4 Let the project dry on a flat surface with good ventilation, such as the top of a refrigerator. Typical drying time is eight hours, and curing normally takes at least 72 hours. It may take longer in conditions of high humidity, or if the application is particularly thick. The paint should become transparent when dry.

Once dry, you may frame your panel for display. To frame, place panel into frame and secure with glazing points, or use Liquid Leading to caulk between the edge of the panel and the back side of the frame. Let caulking dry thoroughly before standing upright.

2 Squeeze paint directly from the bottle. Apply paint first around the perimeter of the leaded area, then fill in the center. Apply paint generously but no higher than the top of the leading.

Using the Modular Technique

1 Place pattern under leading blank. Apply leading evenly. It may help to raise the tip 1" above the work surface to allow leading to drape evenly along pattern lines. Let leading dry at least eight hours. When dry, remove unwanted leading and trim with small scissors.

2 Squeeze paint directly from the bottle. Apply paint first around the perimeter of the leaded area, then fill in the center. Apply paint generously but no higher than the top of the leading. Let dry 24–48 hours.

3 Peel motif from leading blank.

4 Apply motif to surface. Position large elements first then small ones. Be careful not to stretch designs or soil the backs.

5 Make leading strips to connect elements to the window. Apply strips directly to the glass. Separate background into segments as needed with leading strips. Spot-lead any gaps in the leading with liquid leading.

6 Apply background color and texturing directly to the project.

Using the Vertical Technique

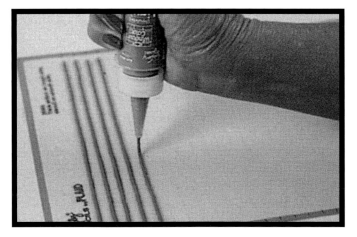

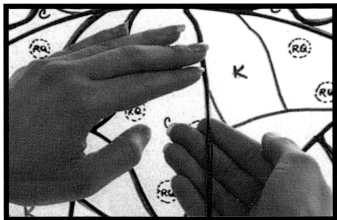

1 Since liquid leading cannot be applied directly to a vertical surface, leading strips need to be prepared and dried before applying to the surface. Squeeze lines of leading (⅛"–³⁄₁₆" diameter) on a leading blank, using lines as guides. Let leading cure thoroughly (at least 72 hours) until strips peel up cleanly.

2 Clean inside and outside of window with glass cleaner. Secure pattern to back of window. Mask-off window sill and edges that touch glass. Tape pattern to outside of window. Apply leading strips to window, following pattern lines. Continue until all pattern lines are covered with leading strips.

3 Working left to right, top to bottom, and one section at a time, apply paint directly onto window. Be certain to paint to the edge, sealing leading strips to the window and avoiding light holes. Use less paint towards the bottom of a section to avoid paint running. Complete an entire section before beginning another.

5 If damage is done to the design from wear, tear, or weather, the area can be removed and recoated. Using a craft knife, score paint along the leading in the damaged section.

4 Using a nut pick, comb wet paint to minimize bubbles and evenly distribute paint. Hold nut pick perpendicular to the glass, and starting at the top, streak tip back and forth until reaching the bottom of the section. Comb similar sections of the pattern in the same direction. Let project dry at least 8 hours.

6 Remove damaged section by peeling color up with your finger. Be certain to remove a complete section at a time. Repeat painting and combing steps. Let dry thoroughly.

Creating Mixes & Shades

Colors can be mixed together thoroughly to form a third color, swirled together within an entire section with a nutpick to create a marbleized look, or a deeper color can be used to shade a design.

Mixing Colors: Pour amount of each color needed into an empty bottle. For example, to make yellowish green use one part Sunny Yellow and two parts Emerald Green. Mix well, then apply from the bottle as usual. If using a texturing technique where the paint is applied with a brush, the paints can be mixed on a palette.

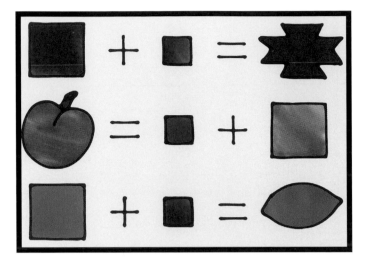

Shading Colors: Place a light and a dark color from the same color family (example light green and dark green) next to each other in the same section. Comb with a toothpick to blend the two together where they meet. This technique is used for flower petals, leaves, and fruits. Do not comb so vigorously that you mix the paints together, simply comb just enough to blend.

Swirling Colors: Create an opalescent look with translucent paints such as Snow White marbleized with one or more paints. Place drops of one paint in an area, then fill in with a second paint. Use the bottle tip, a nutpick, or a toothpick to swirl the two paints. Use translucent paints for both paints and the background will look like opalescent glass.

18

Using a Bevels Mold

1 Squeeze Crystal Clear into mold. Let dry.

3 Place motif on surface. Motif will adhere to glass when applied.

2 Peel dried motif from mold. Trim as needed.

A variety of cut-glass molds are available to create beveled-glass designs.

Projects

Rose Floral

Pictured on page 21

Designed by
Jan Cumber

GATHER THESE SUPPLIES

Glass Art Paints:
Cameo Ivory—03
Crystal Clear—01
Gold Sparkle—19
Kelly Green—08
Magenta Royale—17
Rose Quartz—16

Glass Mediums:
Crackle Medium—49
Etching Medium—44

Other Supplies:
Leading blank
Liquid leading
Nutpick
Soft-bristled paintbrush
Stencil brush

INSTRUCTIONS

Prepare Surface:
1. Refer to Window Preparation on page 10. Prepare window surface.

2. Refer to Working with Patterns on page 10. Place Rose Floral Patterns on pages 22–23 under leading blank.

Lead:
1. Refer to Using the Modular Technique on pages 15–16. Form floral motifs on leading blank with liquid leading. Let dry.

Paint:
1. Refer to Rose Floral Color Guides on pages 22–23. Fill in floral motifs. Using nutpick, even paint. Let dry.

2. Apply floral motifs to window.

3. Refer to Rose Floral Background Guide. Apply Crystal Clear.

4. Using stencil brush, apply Etching Medium. Let dry.

5. Using soft-bristled paintbrush, apply Crackle Medium. Let dry.

Rose Floral Background Guide

20

Rose Floral

Instructions begin
on page 20

Rose Floral Patterns/Color Guide

Enlarge this circular piece 30% more than the other patterns for this window.

19

19

19

19

49 over 01

08

08

Apple Orchard

Pictured on page 25

Designed by
Jacque Hennington

GATHER THESE SUPPLIES

Glass Art Paints:
Cameo Ivory—03
Cocoa Brown—07
Crystal Clear—01
Ivy Green—24
Kelly Green—08
Ruby Red—15
Snow White—02

Other Supplies:
Leading blank
Liquid leading
Nutpick
Premade leading strips

INSTRUCTIONS

Prepare Surface:
1. Refer to Window Preparation on page 10. Prepare window surface.

2. Refer to Working with Patterns on page 10. Place Apple Orchard Patterns on pages 26–27 under leading blank.

Lead:
1. Form checkerboard divisions on glass with premade leading strips.

2. Refer to Using the Modular Technique on pages 15–16. Form apple orchard motifs on leading blank with liquid leading. Let dry.

Paint:
1. Refer to Apple Orchard Color Guides on pages 26–27. Fill in apple orchard motifs. Using nutpick, even paint. Let dry.

2. Apply apple orchard motifs to window.

3. Refer to Apple Orchard Background Guide. Fill in background.

4. Using nutpick, even paint. Do not comb Crystal Clear. Let dry.

Apple Orchard Background Guide

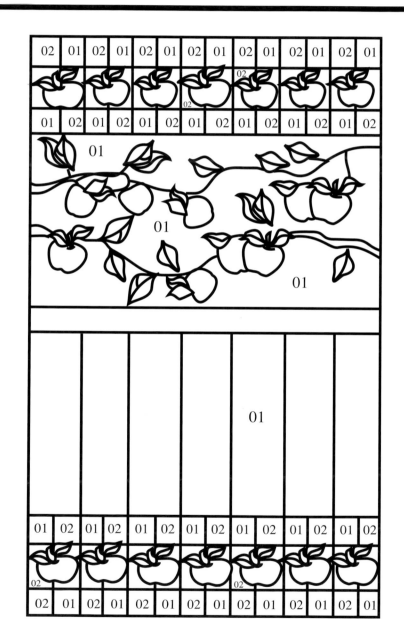

Apple Orchard

Instructions begin on page 24

Apple Orchard Patterns/Color Guide

Rosebud

Instructions begin
on page 30

Rosebud Pattern/Color Guide

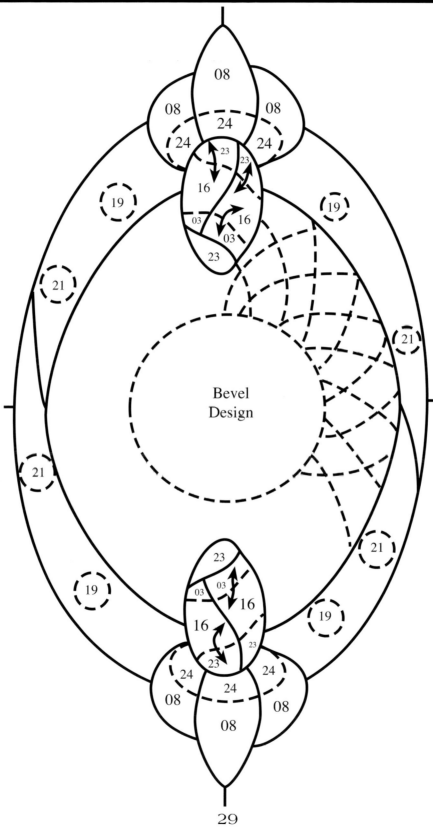

Rosebud

Pictured on page 28

Designed by
Jan Cumber

GATHER THESE SUPPLIES

Glass Art Paints:
   Berry Red—23
   Cameo Ivory—03
   Crystal Clear—01
   Gold Sparkle—19
   Ivy Green—24
   Kelly Green—08
   Rose Quartz—16
   White Pearl—21

Other Supplies:
   Leading blank
   Liquid leading
   Nutpick
   Premade leading strips
   Round bevel mold

INSTRUCTIONS

Prepare Surface:
1. Refer to Window Preparation on page 10. Prepare window surface.

2. Refer to Working with Patterns on page 10. Place Rosebud Pattern on page 29 under leading blank.

Lead:
1. Refer to Using the Modular Technique on pages 15–16. Form rosebud motifs on leading blank with liquid leading. Let dry.

Paint:
1. Refer to Rosebud Color Guide on page 29. Fill in rosebud motifs. Using nutpick, even paint. Let dry.

2. Apply rosebud motifs to window and connect to window edges with premade leading strips.

3. Refer to Using a Bevels Mold on page 19. Using round bevel mold, make bevel design for each cameo center. Let dry.

4. Apply Crystal Clear to window surrounding motifs.

5. Center and adhere bevel designs inside rosebud motifs. Paint lines around bevel design with Crystal Clear.

Empire Oval

Pictured on page 31

Designed by
Carol Smith

GATHER THESE SUPPLIES

Glass Art Paint:
   Crystal Clear—01

Glass Medium:
   Etching Medium—44

Other Supplies:
   Premade leading strips
   Sponge

INSTRUCTIONS

Prepare Surface:
1. Refer to Window Preparation on page 10. Prepare window surface.

2. Refer to Working with Patterns on page 10. Transfer Empire Oval Pattern on page 32 onto window.

Lead:
1. Refer to Using the Vertical Technique on page 16. Outline oval motif with premade leading strips.

Paint:
1. Refer to Empire Oval Color Guide on page 32. Apply Crystal Clear.

2. Using sponge, apply Etching Medium. Let dry.

Empire
Oval
Instructions
begin on
page 30

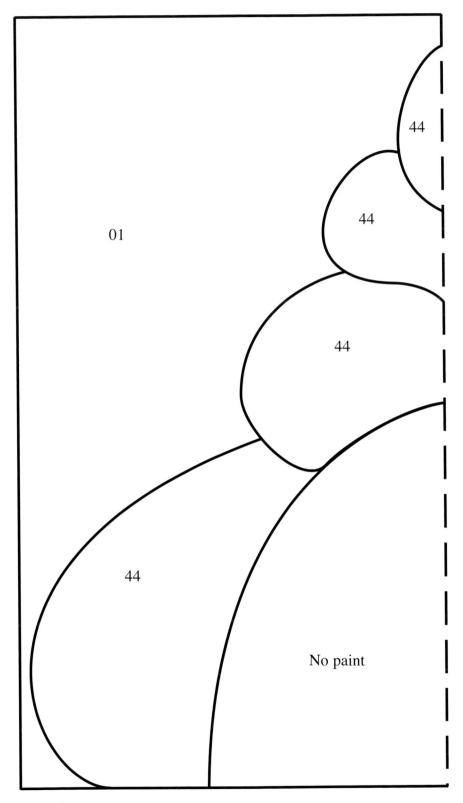

Sensational Iris

Instructions begin
on page 34

Sensational Iris

Pictured on page 33

Designed by
Jan Cumber

GATHER THESE SUPPLIES

Glass Art Paints:
  Amber—20
  Amethyst—14
  Crystal Clear—01
  Kelly Green—08
  Snow White—02
  Sunny Yellow—04

Glass Medium:
  Etching Medium—44

Other Supplies:
  Leading blank
  Liquid leading
  Nutpick
  Premade leading strips
  Stencil brush

INSTRUCTIONS

Prepare Surface:
1. Refer to Window Preparation on page 10. Prepare window surface.

2. Refer to Working with Patterns on page 10. Place Sensational Iris Pattern on page 35 under leading blank.

Lead:
1. Refer to Using the Modular Technique on pages 15–16. Form an iris motif for each window corner on leading blank with liquid leading. Let dry.

Paint:
1. Refer to Sensational Iris Color Guide on page 35. Fill in iris motifs. Using nutpick, even paint. Let dry.

2. Apply iris motifs to window corners. Connect to window edges with premade leading strips.

3. Refer to Sensational Iris Background Guide. Apply Crystal Clear.

4. Using stencil brush, apply Etching Medium. Let dry.

Sensational Iris Background Guide

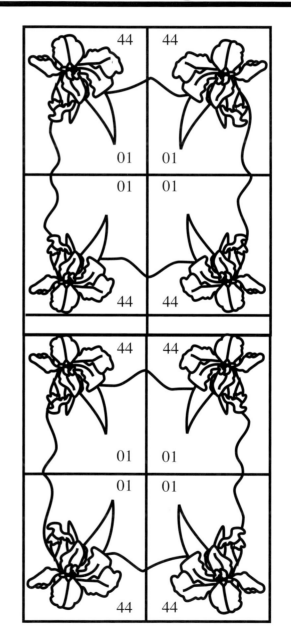

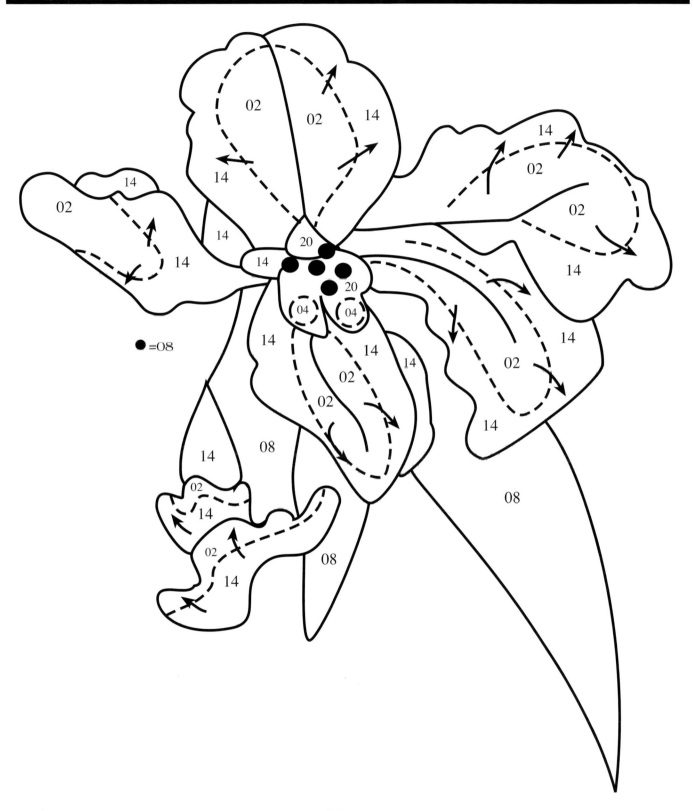

Aquarium

Pictured on page 37

Designed by
Jacque Hennington

GATHER THESE SUPPLIES

Glass Art Paints:
Amber—20
Amethyst—14
Blue Diamond—11
Cameo Ivory—03
Canyon Coral—06
Charcoal Black—18
Cocoa Brown—07
Crystal Clear—01
Ivy Green—24
Kelly Green—08
Orange Poppy—05
Rose Quartz—16
Royal Blue—12
Ruby Red—15
Snow White—02
Sunny Yellow—04
White Pearl—21

Other Supplies:
Leading blank
Liquid leading
Nutpick
Premade leading strips

INSTRUCTIONS

Prepare Surface:
1. Refer to Window Preparation on page 10. Prepare window surface.

2. Refer to Working with Patterns on page 10. Place Aquarium Patterns on pages 38–44 under leading blanks.

Lead:
1. Refer to Using the Modular Technique on pages 15–16. Form aquarium motifs on leading blank with liquid leading. Let dry.

Paint:
1. Refer to Aquarium Color Guides on pages 38–44. Fill in design. Using nutpick, even paint. Let dry.

2. Apply aquarium motifs to window.

3. Make grass, waterlines, rocks, and ocean floor lines with premade leading strips.

4. Refer to Aquarium Background Guide. Fill in background.

Aquarium Background Guide

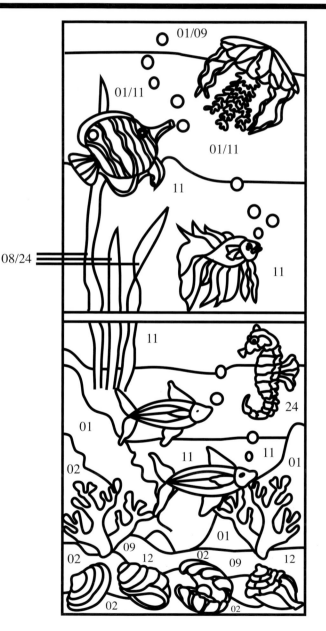

Aquarium
Instructions
begin on
page 36

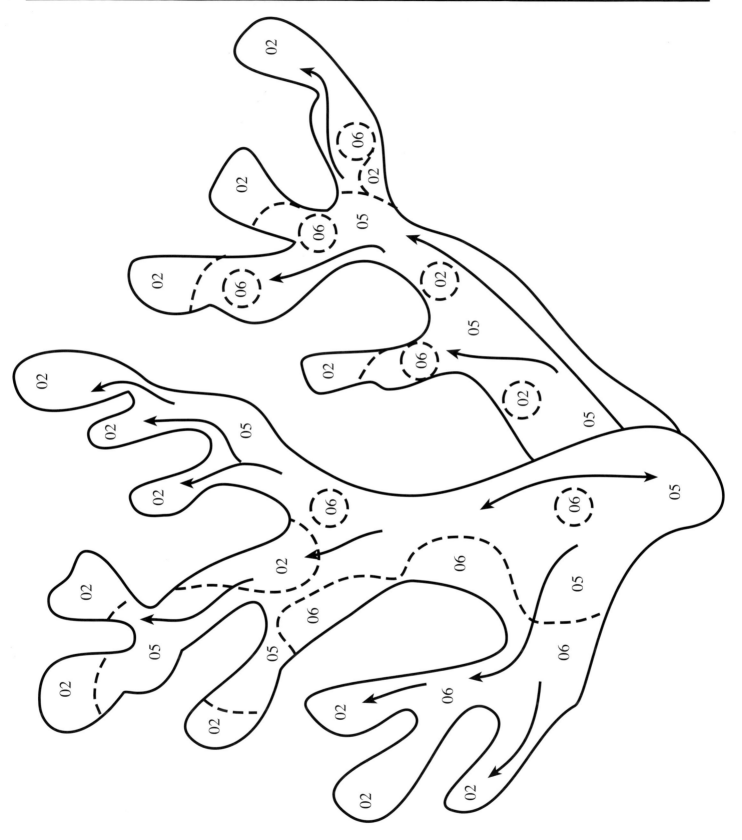

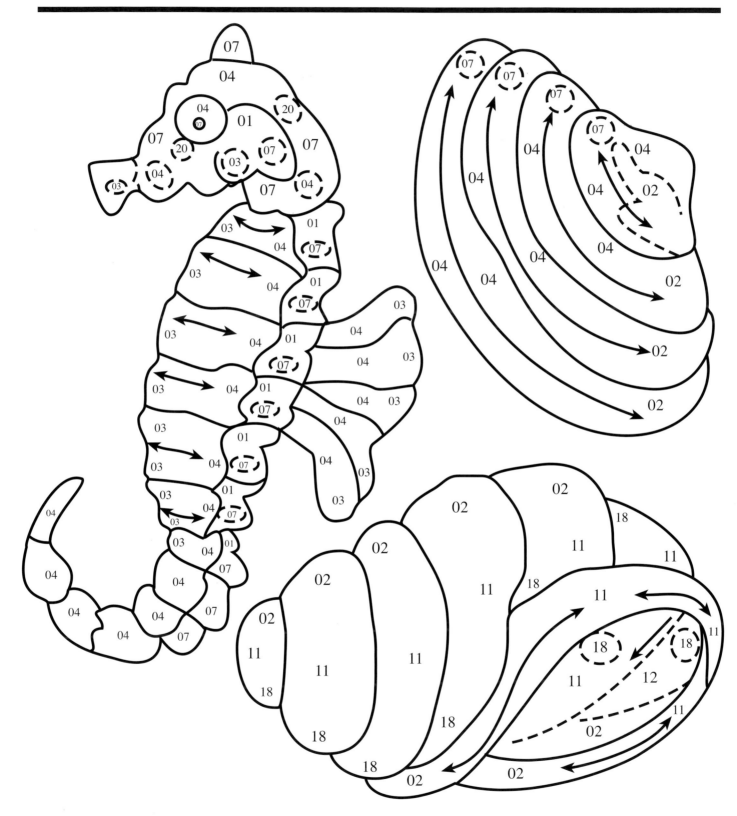

Aquarium Patterns/Color Guide

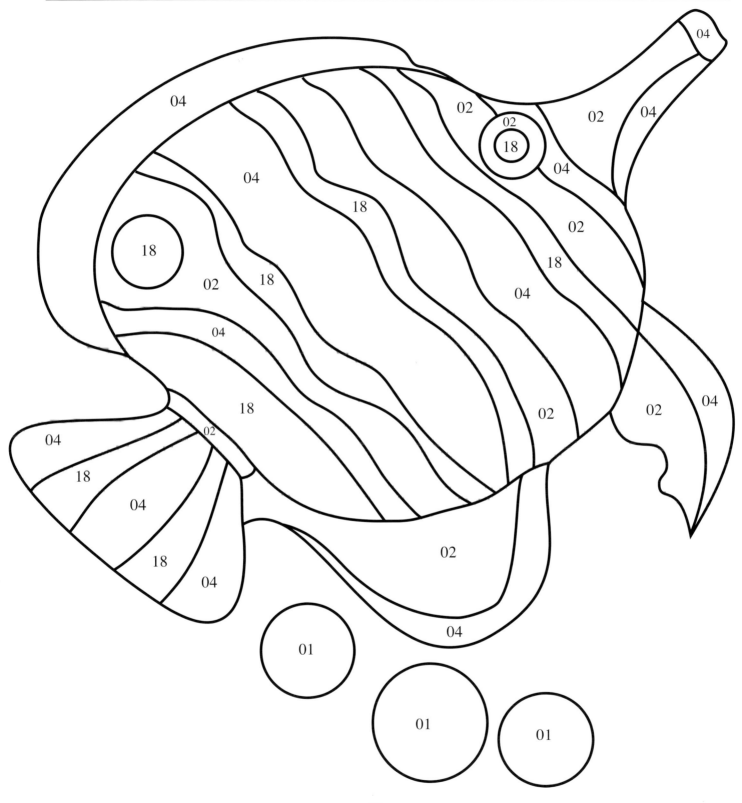

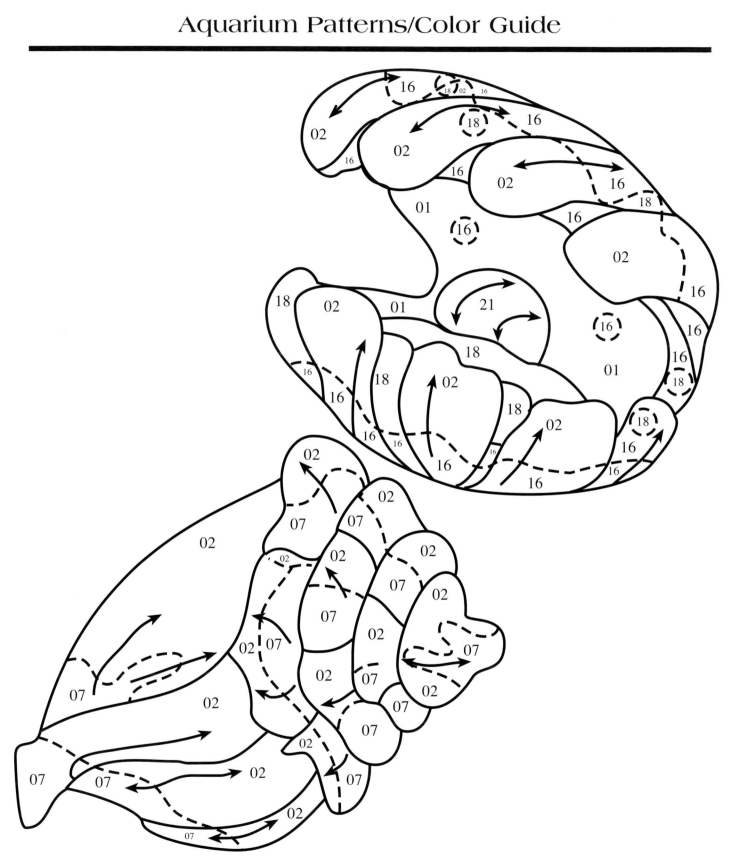

Fruit & Swag

Instructions begin
on page 46

Fruit & Swag

Pictured on page 45

Designed by
Carol Smith

GATHER THESE SUPPLIES

Glass Art Paints:
Amber—20
Amethyst—14
Berry Red—23
Canyon Coral—06
Crystal Clear—01
Denim Blue—10
Ivy Green—24
Kelly Green—08
Magenta Royale—17
Ruby Red—15
Snow White—02

Other Supplies:
Leading blank
Liquid leading
Nutpick
Premade leading strips

INSTRUCTIONS

Prepare Surface:
1. Refer to Window Preparation on page 10. Prepare window surface.

2. Refer to Working with Patterns on page 10. Place Fruit & Swag Patterns on pages 47–49 under leading blank.

Lead:
1. Refer to Using the Modular Technique on pages 15–16. Form fruit and swag motifs on leading blank with liquid leading. Let dry.

Paint:
1. Refer to Fruit & Swag Color Guides on pages 47–49. Fill in fruit and swag motifs. Using nutpick, even paint. Do not comb Crystal Clear. Let dry.

2. Apply fruit and swag motifs to window.

3. Connect fruit and swag motifs randomly to window frame with premade leading strips.

4. Fill between fruit and swag motifs and window frame with Crystal Clear. Let dry.

In this kitchen, the swags were used across the top of the window and the narrow swags were used on the sides. Use one of two motifs to tie them together: the fruit, shown in this kitchen window, or roses.

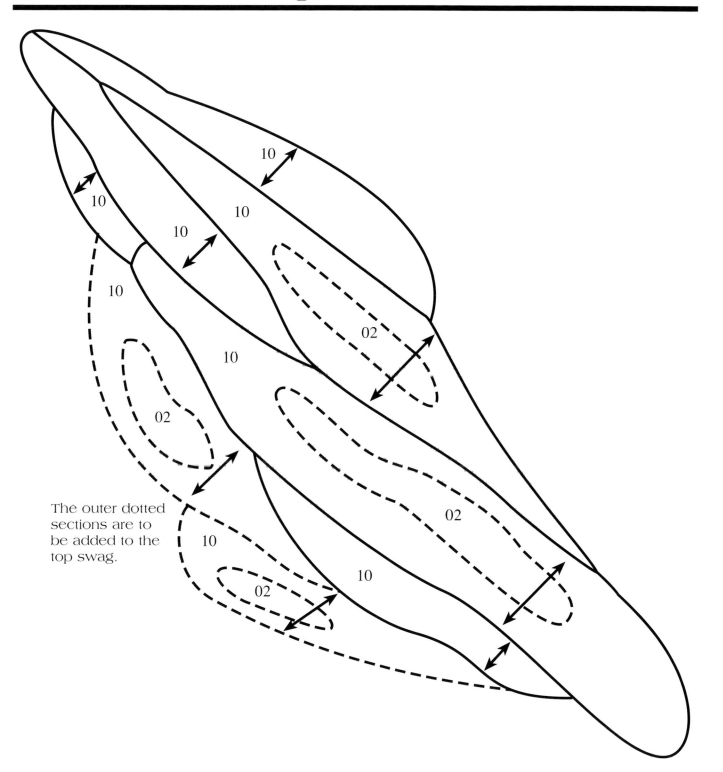

The outer dotted sections are to be added to the top swag.

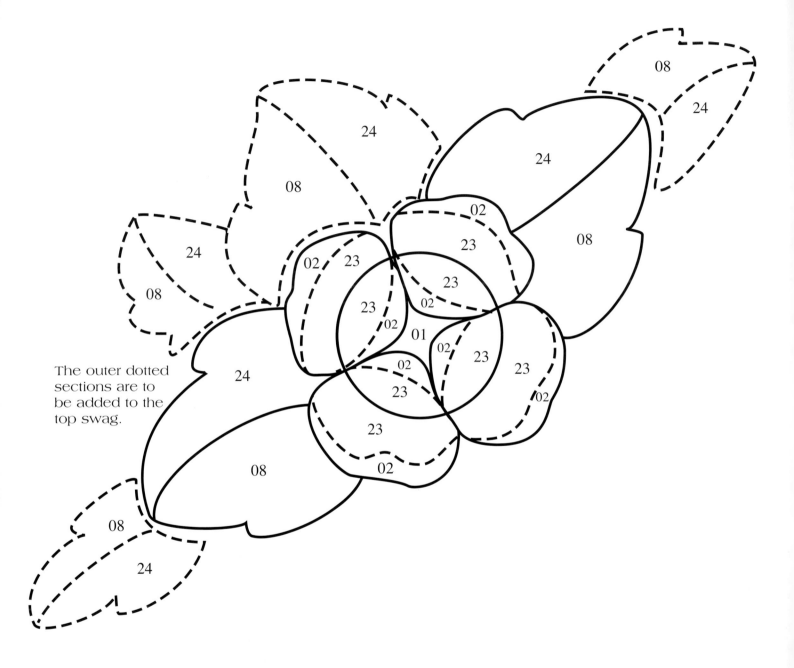

The outer dotted sections are to be added to the top swag.

Fruit & Swag Pattern/Color Guide

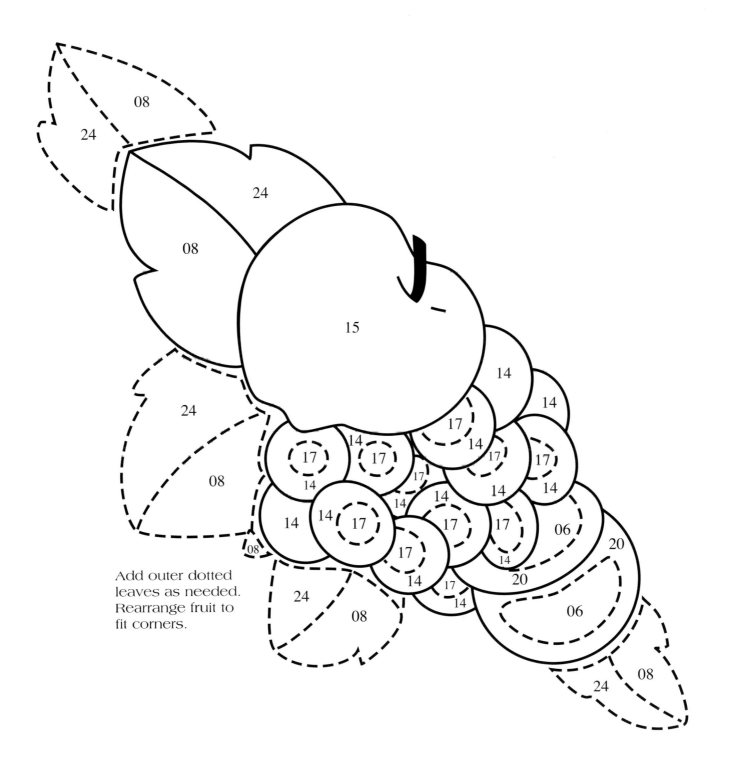

Add outer dotted leaves as needed. Rearrange fruit to fit corners.

Ribbon Corner

Pictured on page 51

Designed by
Carol Smith

GATHER THESE SUPPLIES

Glass Art Paints:
   Amethyst—14
   Crystal Clear—01
   Emerald Green—09
   Kelly Green—08
   Magenta Royale—17

Glass Medium:
   Etching Medium—44

Other Supplies:
   Nutpick
   Premade leading strips
   Sponge

INSTRUCTIONS

Prepare Surface:
1. Refer to Window Preparation on page 10. Prepare window surface.

2. Refer to Working with Patterns on page 10. Transfer Ribbon Corner Pattern on page 58 onto window.

Lead:
1. Refer to Using the Vertical Technique on page 16. Outline ribbon motif with premade leading strips.

Paint:
1. Refer to Ribbon Corner Background Guide. Apply Crystal Clear.

2. Using sponge, apply Etching Medium. Let dry.

3. Refer to Ribbon Corner Color Guide on page 52. Fill in design. Using nutpick, even paint. Do not comb Crystal Clear. Let dry.

Ribbon Corner Background Guide

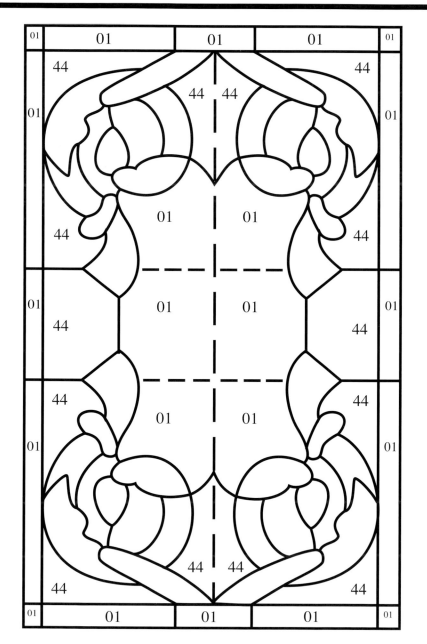

Ribbon Corner

Instructions begin on page 50

Ribbon Corner Pattern/Color Guide

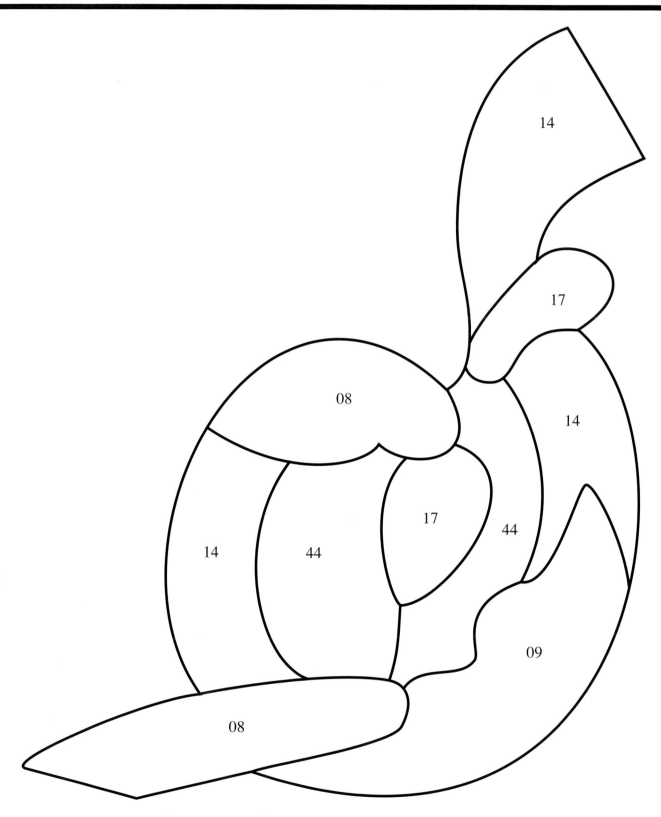

Summer Rose
Instructions begin
on page 54

Summer Rose

Pictured on pages 53 & 55

Designed by
Carol Smith

GATHER THESE SUPPLIES

Glass Art Paints:
  Amethyst—14
  Clear Frost—22
  Crystal Clear—01
  Ivy Green—24
  Rose Quartz—16
  Snow White—02
  Sunny Yellow—04

Other Supplies:
  Nutpick
  Premade leading strips
  Soft-bristled paintbrush

INSTRUCTIONS

Prepare Surface:
1. Refer to Window Preparation on page 10. Prepare window surface.

2. Refer to Working with Patterns on page 10. Transfer Summer Rose Patterns on pages 56–57 onto window.

Lead:
1. Refer to Using the Vertical Technique on page 16. Outline motif with premade leading strips. Add vertical stripes to top and bottom of window.

Paint:
1. Refer to Summer Rose Background Guide and Summer Rose Color Guides on pages 56–57. Fill in design.

2. Using nutpick, even paint. Do not comb Crystal Clear. Let dry.

3. Using soft-bristled paintbrush, apply Clear Frost.

Summer Rose Background Guide

02	16	02	16	02	16	02	16

The Summer Rose design and its inverted image were enlarged to fit the width of these bedroom windows. Stripes were added to the top and bottom to coordinate with coverlet and upholstery fabric. Flower colors from the pillow covers were used to paint the roses.

Summer Rose Pattern/Color Guide

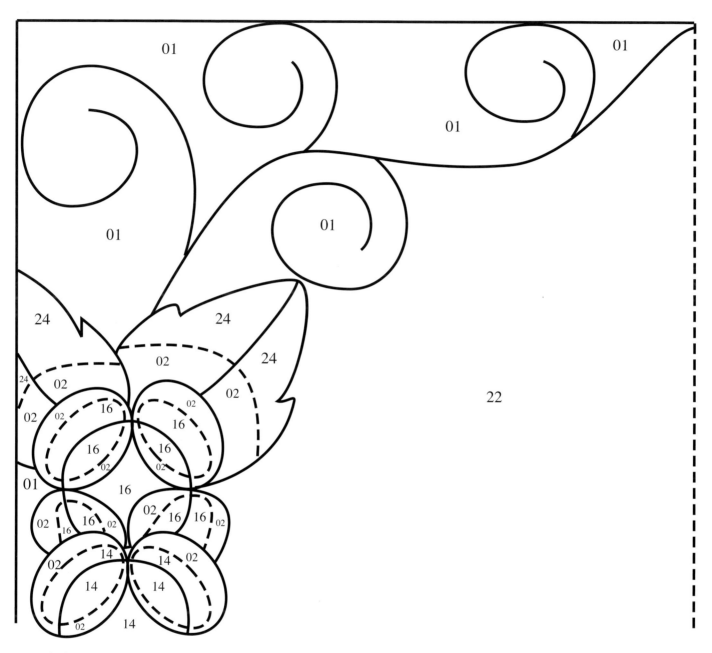

Top left corner
Mirror image to create
top right corner.

Summer Rose Pattern/Color Guide

Bottom left corner
Mirror image to create
bottom right corner.

Rooster in the Garden

Pictured on page 59

Designed by
Carol Smith

GATHER THESE SUPPLIES

Glass Art Paints:
Amber—20
Berry Red—23
Cocoa Brown—07
Crystal Clear—01
Denim Blue—10
Ivy Green—24
Kelly Green—08
Lime Green—35
Snow White—02
Sunny Yellow—04

Glass Medium:
Etching Medium—44

Other Supplies:
China marker
Leading blank
Liquid leading
Nutpick
Premade leading strips
Ruler
Stencil brush

INSTRUCTIONS

Prepare Surface:
1. Refer to Window Preparation on page 10. Prepare window surface.

2. Refer to Working with Patterns on page 10. Place Rooster in the Garden Patterns on pages 60–61 under leading blank.

Lead:
1. Form oval on window with premade leading strips.

2. Using ruler and china marker, mark 2" squares around oval. Outline squares with premade leading strips.

3. Refer to Using the Modular Technique on pages 15–16. Form garden motifs on leading blank with liquid leading. Let dry.

Paint:
1. Refer to Rooster in the Garden Color Guides on pages 60–61. Fill in garden motifs. Using nutpick, even paint. Let dry.

2. Apply garden motifs to window.

3. Refer to photograph on page 59. Fill in area outside vegetables with Crystal Clear.

4. Refer to Rooster in the Garden Background Guide. Fill in squares.

5. Using stencil brush, apply Etching Medium in center of window. Using nutpick, even paint. Do not comb Crystal Clear. Let dry.

Rooster in the Garden Background Guide

10	02
02	10
10	02

Rooster in the Garden

Instructions begin on page 58

Rooster in the Garden Pattern/Color Guide

Rooster in the Garden Pattern/Color Guide

Kites & Kittens

Pictured on page 63

Designed by
Jacque Hennington

GATHER THESE SUPPLIES

Glass Art Paints:
Amber—20
Berry Red—23
Cameo Ivory—03
Charcoal Black—18
Cocoa Brown—07
Crystal Clear—01
Denim Blue—10
Kelly Green—08
Lime Green—35
Snow White—02

Glass Medium:
Etching Medium—44

Other Supplies:
China marker
Leading blank
Liquid leading
Nutpick
Premade leading strips
Ruler
Stencil brush

INSTRUCTIONS

Prepare Surface:
1. Refer to Window Preparation on page 10. Prepare window surface.

2. Using ruler and china marker, mark off borders in staggered rectangles approximately 4" long and 1¼" wide.

3. Refer to Using the Vertical Technique of page 16. Outline rectangle border with premade leading strips.

4. Refer to Working with Patterns on page 10. Place Kites & Kittens Patterns on pages 64–66 under leading blank.

Lead:
1. Refer to Using the Modular Technique on pages 15–16. Form kites and kittens motifs on leading blank with liquid leading. Let dry.

Paint:
1. Refer to Kites & Kittens Color Guides on pages 64–66. Fill in kites and kittens motifs. Using nutpick, even paint. Let dry.

2. Apply kite and kitten motifs to window.

3. Refer to photograph on page 63. Randomly form clouds, and horizontal lines across windows, and kite strings with premade leading strips.

4. Refer to Kites & Kittens Background Guide. Using stencil brush, apply Etching Medium.

5. Fill in remaining background sections. Using nutpick, even paints. Do not comb Crystal Clear. Let dry.

Kites & Kittens Background Guide

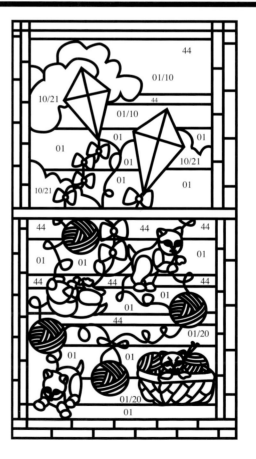

Kites & Kittens
Instructions begin
on page 62

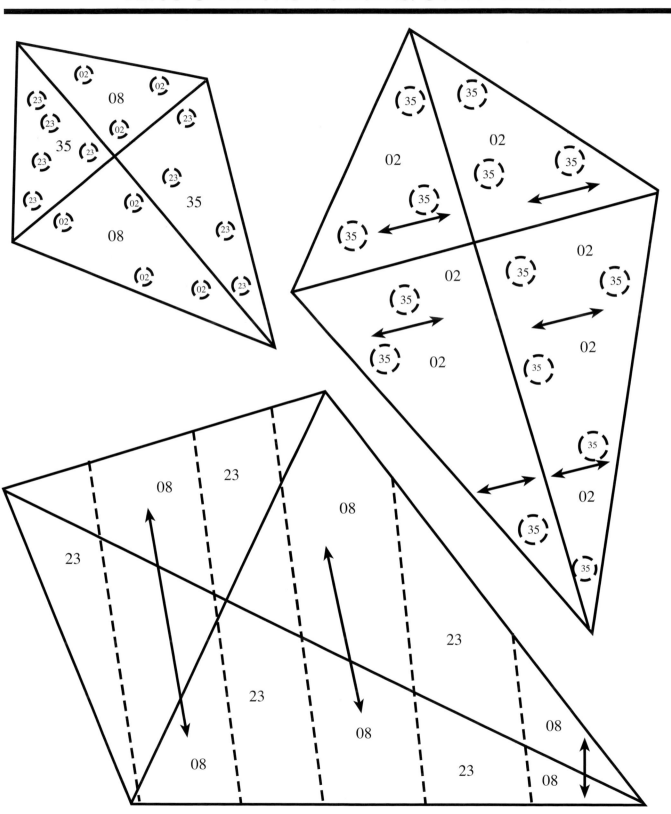

Kites & Kittens Patterns/Color Guide

Kites & Kittens Patterns/Color Guide

French Manor
Instructions begin
on page 68

French Manor

Pictured on page 67

Designed by
Carol Smith

GATHER THESE SUPPLIES

Glass Art Paints:
Amber—20
Cameo Ivory—03
Crystal Clear—01
Gold Sparkle—19
Snow White—02

Glass Medium:
Etching Medium—44

Other Supplies:
China marker
Gold Metallic liquid leading
Gold premade leading strips
Leading blank
Nutpick
Round bevel mold
Ruler
Stencil brush

INSTRUCTIONS

Prepare Surface:
1. Refer to Window Preparation on page 10. Prepare window surface.

2. Refer to Working with Patterns on page 10. Place Fleur-de-lis Pattern on page 71 under leading blank.

Lead:
1. Refer to Using the Modular Technique on pages 15–16. Form fleur-de-lis motif with liquid leading. Let dry.

French Manor Pattern/Color Guide

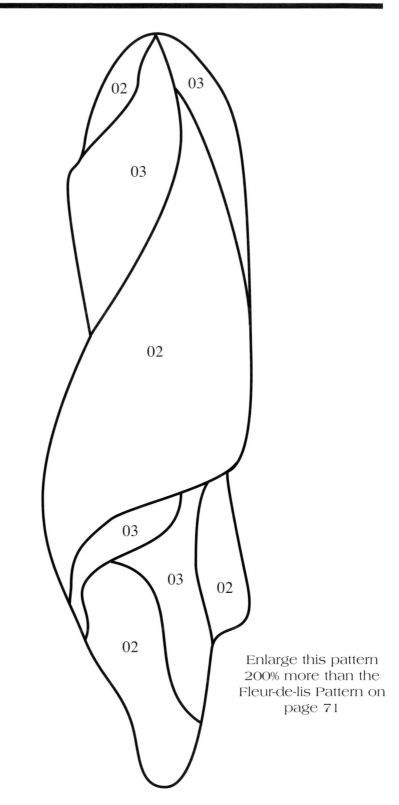

Enlarge this pattern 200% more than the Fleur-de-lis Pattern on page 71

French Manor Pattern/Color Guide

2. Refer to Using the Vertical Technique on page 16. Transfer French Manor Patterns on pages 68–70 onto window.

3. Outline swag motifs with premade leading strips.

4. Using china marker and ruler, mark off window center into 6" x 6" squares.

5. Refer to Using a Bevels Mold on page 19. Using round bevel mold, make bevel design for each intersection. Let dry.

Paint:
1. Refer to Fleur-de-lis Color Guide on page 71. Fill in fleur-de-lis motif. Using nutpick, even paint. Let dry.

2. Refer to French Manor Color Guides on pages 68–70. Fill in French manor motifs. Using nutpick, even paint. Let dry.

3. Apply fleur-de-lis motifs to top of window.

4. Apply Crystal Clear to all squares on window. Let dry.

5. Using stencil brush, apply Etching Medium to all squares. Let dry.

6. Apply one bevel design to each intersection of lines.

7. Connect bevel designs with premade leading strips.

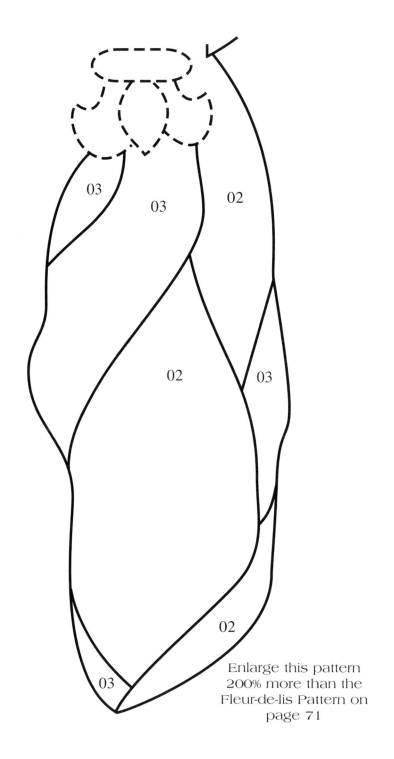

Enlarge this pattern 200% more than the Fleur-de-lis Pattern on page 71

69

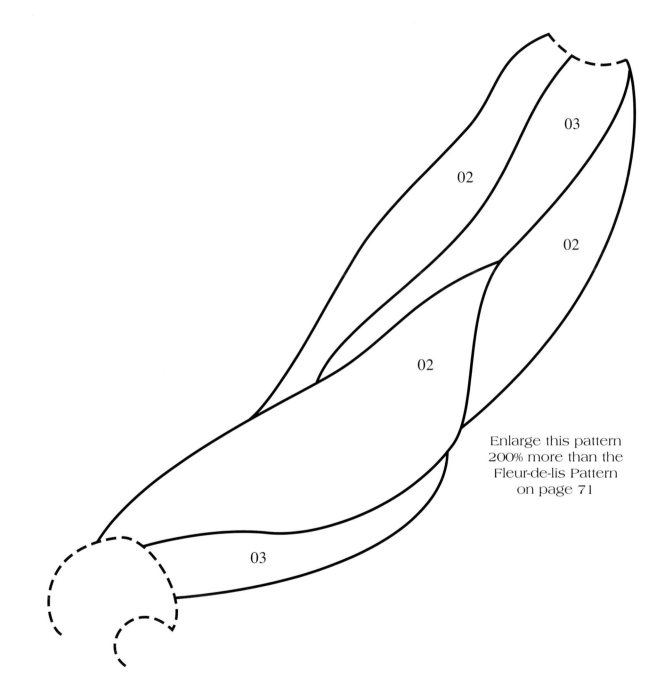

03

02

02

02

03

Enlarge this pattern
200% more than the
Fleur-de-lis Pattern
on page 71

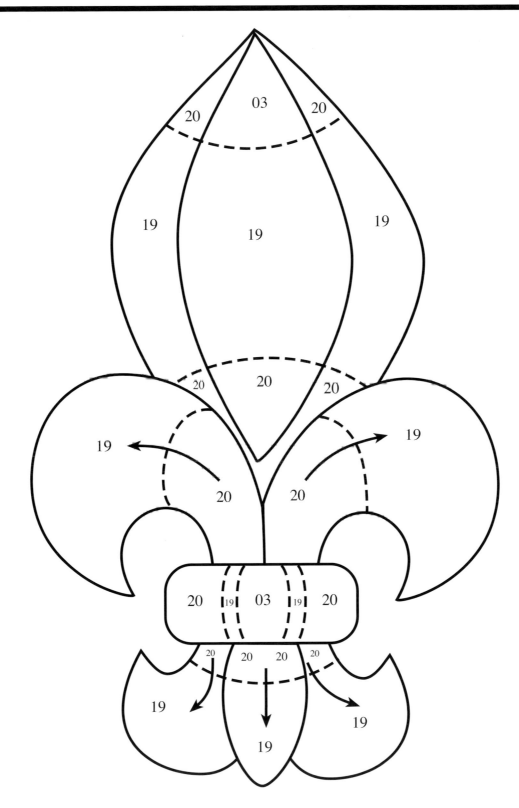

Cozy Bay

Designed by
Carol Smith

GATHER THESE SUPPLIES

Glass Art Paints:
Berry Red—23
Champagne—94
Crystal Clear—01
Ivy Green—24

Glass Medium:
Etching Medium—44

Other Supplies:
Nutpick
Premade leading strips
Sponge

INSTRUCTIONS

Prepare Surface:
1. Refer to Window Preparation on page 10. Prepare window surface.

2. Refer to Working with Patterns on page 10. Transfer Cozy Bay Patterns on pages 74–75 onto window.

Lead:
1. Refer to Using the Vertical Technique on page 16. Form cozy bay motifs and connect pieces with premade leading strips.

Paint:
1. Refer to Cozy Bay Color Guides on pages 74–75. Fill in cozy bay motifs. Using nutpick, even paint. Do not comb Crystal Clear. Let dry.

2. Refer to Cozy Bay Background Guide on page 75. Fill in background.

3. Using sponge, apply Etching Medium. Let dry.

Cozy Bay

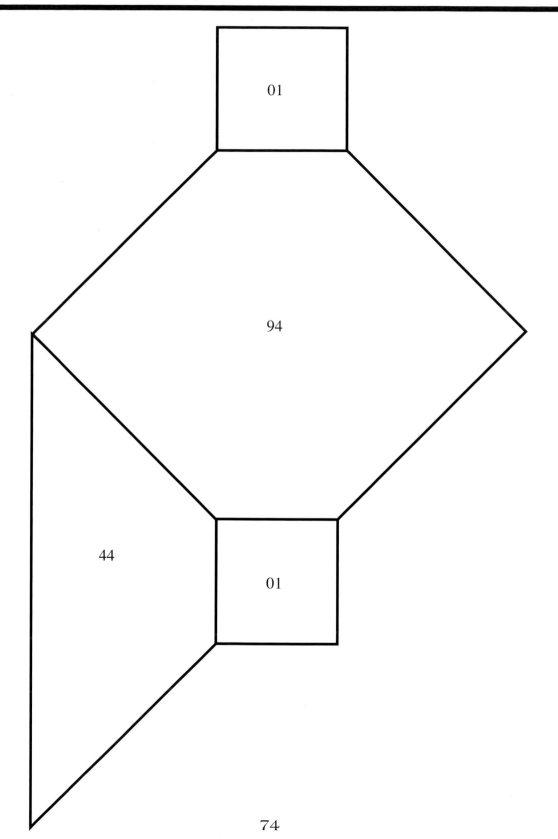

Cozy Bay Pattern/Color Guide

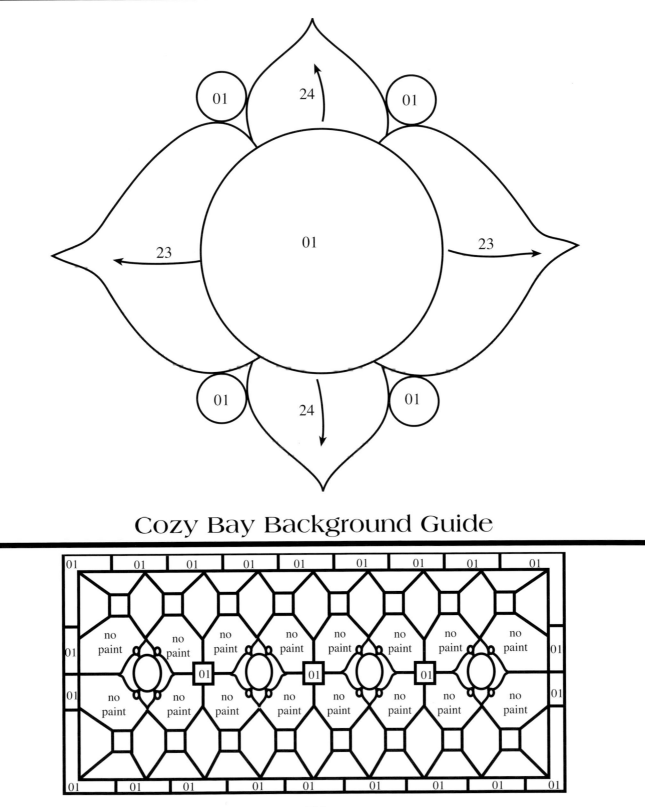

Cozy Bay Background Guide

Classic Cameo

Designed by
Carol Smith

GATHER THESE SUPPLIES

Glass Art Paints:
Cameo Ivory—03
Crystal Clear—01
Kelly Green—08
Rose Quartz—16

Glass Medium:
Etching Medium—44

Other Supplies:
Nutpick
Premade leading strips
Sponge

INSTRUCTIONS

Prepare Surface:
1. Refer to Window Preparation on page 10. Prepare window surface.

2. Refer to Working with Patterns on page 10. Transfer Classic Cameo Pattern on page 78 onto window.

Lead:
1. Refer to Using the Vertical Technique on page 16. Outline cameo motif with premade leading strips.

Paint:
1. Refer to Classic Cameo Background Guide. Apply Crystal Clear.

2. Using sponge, apply Etching Medium. Let dry.

3. Refer to Classic Cameo Color Guide on page 78. Fill in design. Using nutpick, even paint. Let dry.

Classic Cameo Background Guide

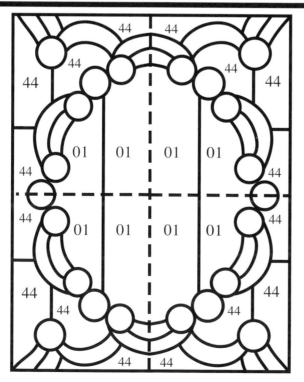

76

Classic Cameo

Classic Cameo Pattern/Color Guide

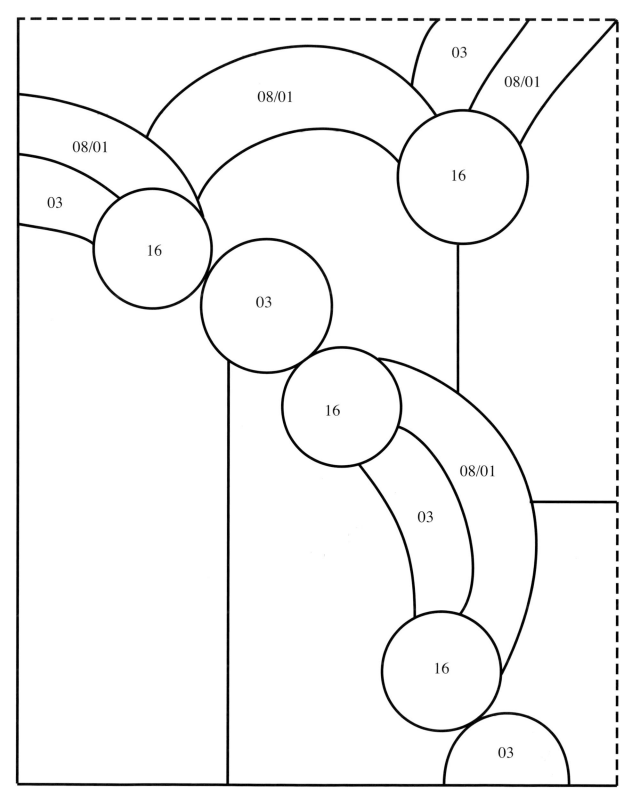

Lemon Delight

Instructions begin
on page 80

Lemon Delight

Pictured on page 79

Designed by
Jacque Hennington

GATHER THESE SUPPLIES

Glass Art Paints:
  Crystal Clear—01
  Emerald Green—09
  Royal Blue—12
  Snow White—02
  Sunny Yellow—04

Other Supplies:
  Leading blank
  Liquid leading
  Nutpick
  Premade leading strips

INSTRUCTIONS

Prepare Surface:
1. Refer to Window Preparation on page 10. Prepare window surface.

2. Refer to Working with Patterns on page 10. Place Lemon Delight Patterns on pages 81–83 under leading blank.

Lead:
1. Refer to Using the Modular Technique on pages 15–16. Form lemon motifs on leading blank with liquid leading. Use mirror image of some of the lemons so not all the designs look alike. Let dry.

Paint:
1. Refer to Lemon Delight Color Guides on pages 81–83. Fill in motifs. Using nutpick, even paint. Let dry.

2. Refer to Using the Vertical Technique on page 16. Refer to Lemon Delight Background Guide. Create a simple border with premade leading strips.

3. Apply paints to border. Even paint. Let dry.

4. Apply lemon motifs to window. Connect designs with premade leading strips.

5. Fill in area around lemon motifs with Crystal Clear. Let dry.

Lemon Delight
Background Guide

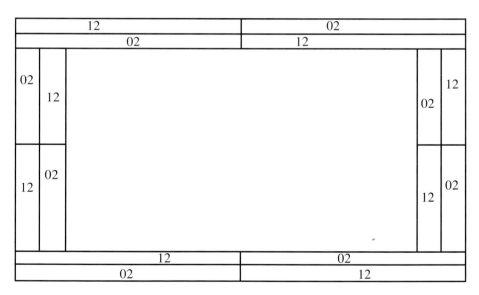

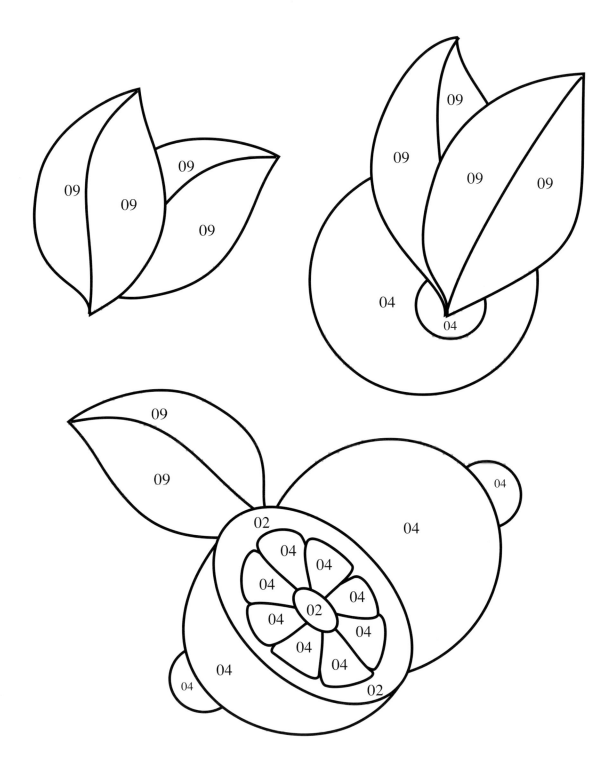

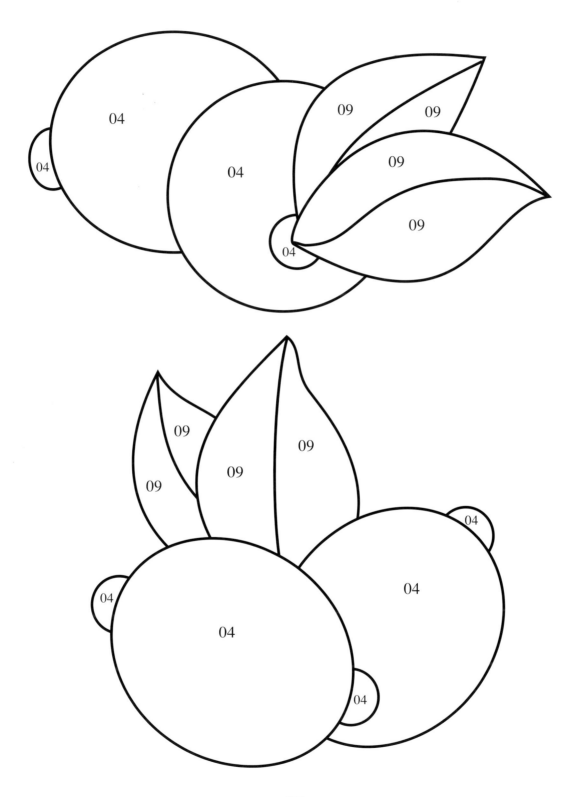

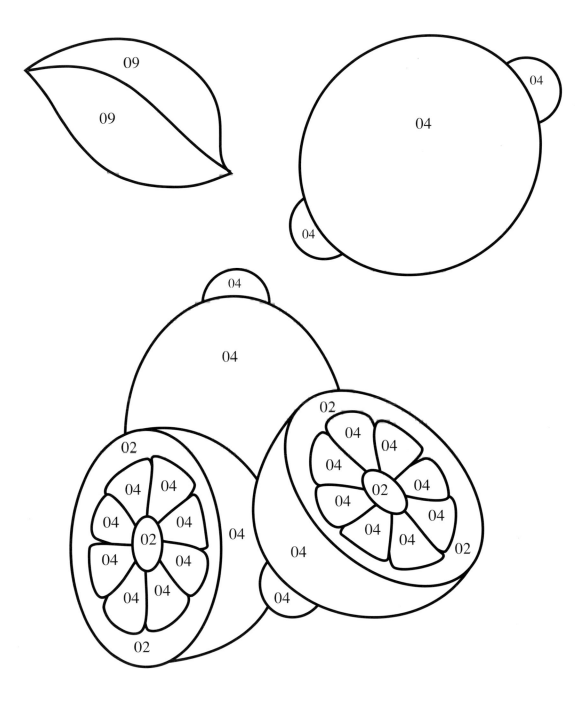

English Ivy

Pictured on page 85

Designed by
Jacque Hennington

GATHER THESE SUPPLIES

Glass Art Paints:
  Cameo Ivory—03
  Crystal Clear—01
  Kelly Green—08

Other Supplies:
  Leading blank
  Liquid leading
  Nutpick
  Premade leading strips

INSTRUCTIONS

Prepare Surface:
1. Refer to Window Preparation on page 10. Prepare window surface.

2. Refer to Working with Patterns on page 10. Place English Ivy Patterns under leading blank.

Lead:
1. Refer to Using the Modular Technique on pages 15–16. Form ivy motifs on leading blank with liquid leading. Let dry.

Paint:
1. Refer to English Ivy Color Guide. Fill in design. Using nutpick, even paint. Let dry.

2. Apply motifs to window, placing larger leaves first and using smaller leaves and tendrils to fill gaps and tie design together.

3. Add tendrils and lines connecting leaves to window sills with premade leading strips.

4. Apply Crystal Clear to window surrounding motifs. Let dry.

English Ivy Patterns/Color Guide

English Ivy

Instructions begin
on page 84

Magnolia & Azalea

Designed by
Jan Cumber

GATHER THESE SUPPLIES

Glass Art Paints:
　Amber—20
　Cameo Ivory—03
　Cocoa Brown—07
　Crystal Clear—01
　Ivy Green—24
　Kelly Green—08
　Magenta Royal—17
　Snow White—02

Glass Mediums:
　Etching Medium—44

Other Supplies:
　Leading blank
　Liquid leading
　Nutpick
　Premade leading strips
　Stencil brush

INSTRUCTIONS

Prepare Surface:
1. Refer to Window Preparation on page 10. Prepare window surface.

2. Refer to Working with Patterns on page 10. Place Magnolia & Azalea Patterns on pages 88–89 under leading blank.

Lead:
1. Refer to Using the Modular Technique on pages 15–16. Form flower motifs on leading blank with liquid leading. Use mirror images of azalea blossom for variety. Let dry.

Paint:
1. Refer to Magnolia & Azalea Color Guides on pages 88–89. Fill in flower motifs. Using nutpick, even paint. Let dry.

2. Apply flower motifs to window.

3. Refer to Using the Vertical Technique on page 16. Outline branches and connecting lines with premade leading strips.

4. Apply Crystal Clear to background.

5. Using stencil brush, apply Etching Medium to inside of flower motifs. Let dry.

Seashell

Pictured on page 91

Designed by
Jan Cumber

GATHER THESE SUPPLIES

Glass Art Paints:
    Cameo Ivory—03
    Canyon Coral—06
    Charcoal Black—18
    Clear Frost—22
    Cocoa Brown—07
    Crystal Clear—01
    Magenta Royale—17
    Snow White—02

Other Supplies:
    Leading blank
    Liquid leading
    Nutpick
    Premade leading strips
    Soft-bristled paintbrush

INSTRUCTIONS

Prepare Surface:
1. Refer to Window Preparation on page 10. Prepare window surface.

2. Refer to Working with Patterns on page 10. Place Seashell Pattern on page 92 under leading blank.

Lead:
1. Refer to Using the Modular Technique on pages 15–16. Form seashell motif as one unit on leading blank with liquid leading. Let dry.

Paint:
1. Refer to Seashell Color Guide on page 92. Fill in seashell motif. Using nutpick, even paint. Let dry.

2. Apply seashell motif to window. Connect top and bottom pieces together with premade leading strips.

3. Connect seashell motif to window edges with premade leading strips.

4. Refer to Seashell Background Guide. Apply Crystal Clear.

5. Using soft-bristled paintbrush, apply Clear Frost. Let dry.

Seashell Background Guide

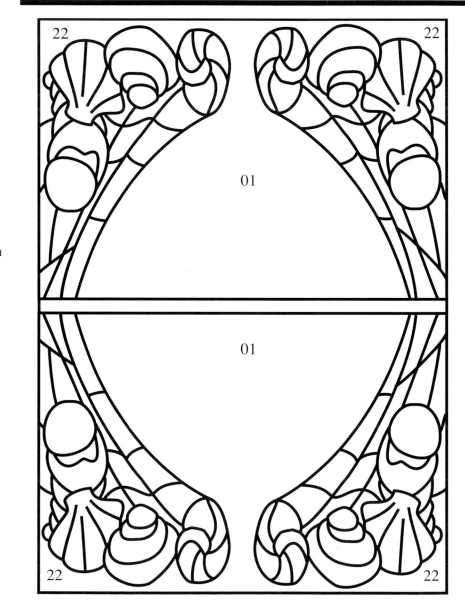

Seashell
Instructions begin
on page 90

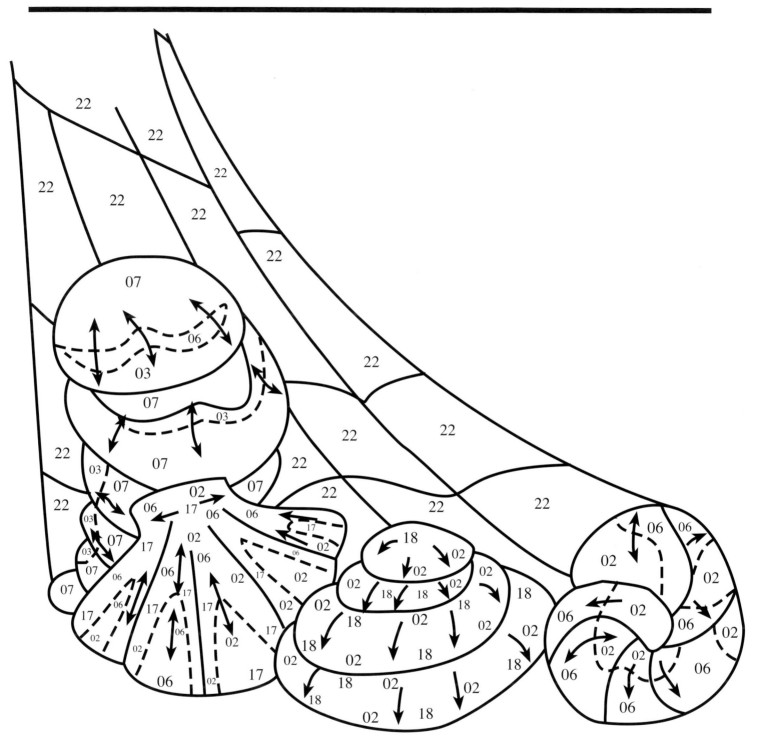

Iris Side Panel
Instructions begin
on page 94

Iris Side Panel

Pictured on page 93

Designed by
Carol Smith

GATHER THESE SUPPLIES

Glass Art Paints:
Amber—20
Amethyst—14
Crystal Clear—01
Emerald Green—09
Ivy Green—24
Kelly Green—08

Other Supplies:
Nutpick
Premade leading strips
Ruler

INSTRUCTIONS

Prepare Surface:
1. Refer to Window Preparation on page 10. Prepare window surface.

2. Refer to Working with Patterns on page 10. Transfer Iris Side Panel Patterns on pages 95–96 onto window.

Lead:
1. Refer to Using the Vertical Technique on page 16. Outline iris motif with premade leading strips.

Paint:
1. Refer to Iris Side Panel Background Guide. Apply Crystal Clear. Let dry.

2. Refer to Iris Side Panel Color Guides on pages 95–96. Fill in design. Using nutpick, even paint. Let dry.

Iris Side Panel Background Guide

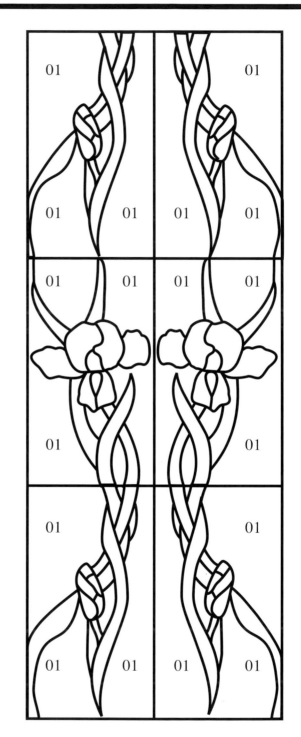

Iris Side Panel Pattern/Color Guide

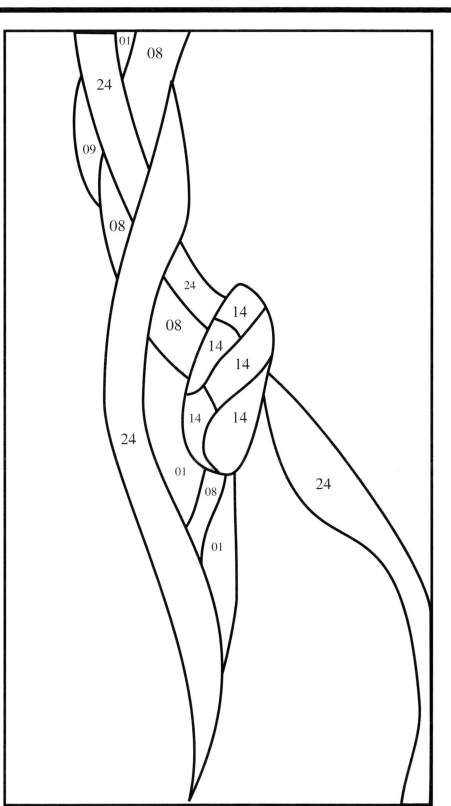

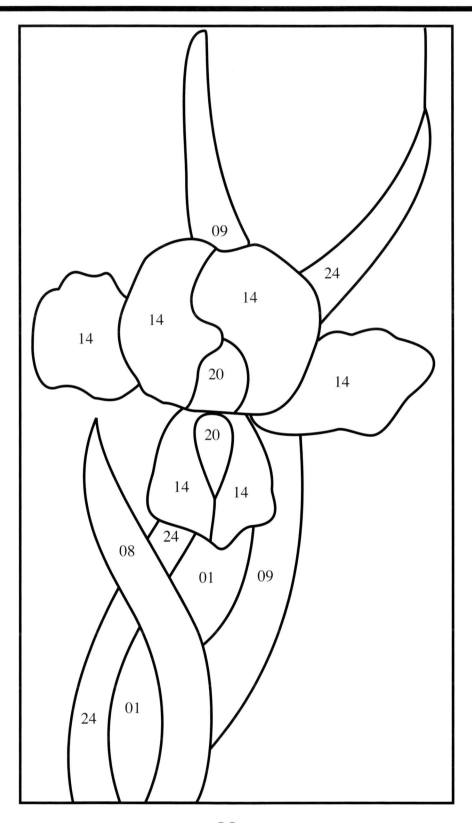

Musical
Instruments
Instructions begin
on page 98

Musical Instruments

Pictured on page 97

Designed by
Carol Smith

GATHER THESE SUPPLIES

Glass Art Paints:
Amber—20
Amethyst—14
Crystal Clear—01
Gold Sparkle—19
Ivy Green—24
Snow White—02
White Pearl—21

Glass Medium:
Etching Medium—44

Other Supplies:
China marker
Leading blank
Liquid leading
Nutpick
Premade leading strips
Ruler
Stencil brush

INSTRUCTIONS

Prepare Surface:
1. Refer to Window Preparation on page 10. Prepare window surface.

2. Refer to Working with Patterns on page 10. Place Musical Instruments Patterns on page 99 under leading blank.

Lead:
1. Refer to Using the Modular Technique on pages 15–16. Form piano and note motifs on leading blank with liquid leading. Let dry.

2. Refer to Using the Vertical Technique on page 16. Refer to Musical Instruments Patterns on pages 100–101. Outline harp and oval motifs with premade leading strips.

Paint:
1. Refer to Musical Instruments Color Guide on page 99. Fill in piano and note motifs. Using nutpick, even paint. Let dry.

2. Apply piano and note motifs to window.

3. Refer to Musical Instruments Color Guides on pages 100–101. Fill in design.

4. Using china marker and ruler, mark 1½" border. Add radiating lines with premade leading strips.

5. Refer to Musical Instruments Background Guides. Using stencil brush, apply Etching Medium. Using nutpick, even paint.

6. Fill in remaining design. Leave border clear. Let dry.

Musical Instruments Background Guides

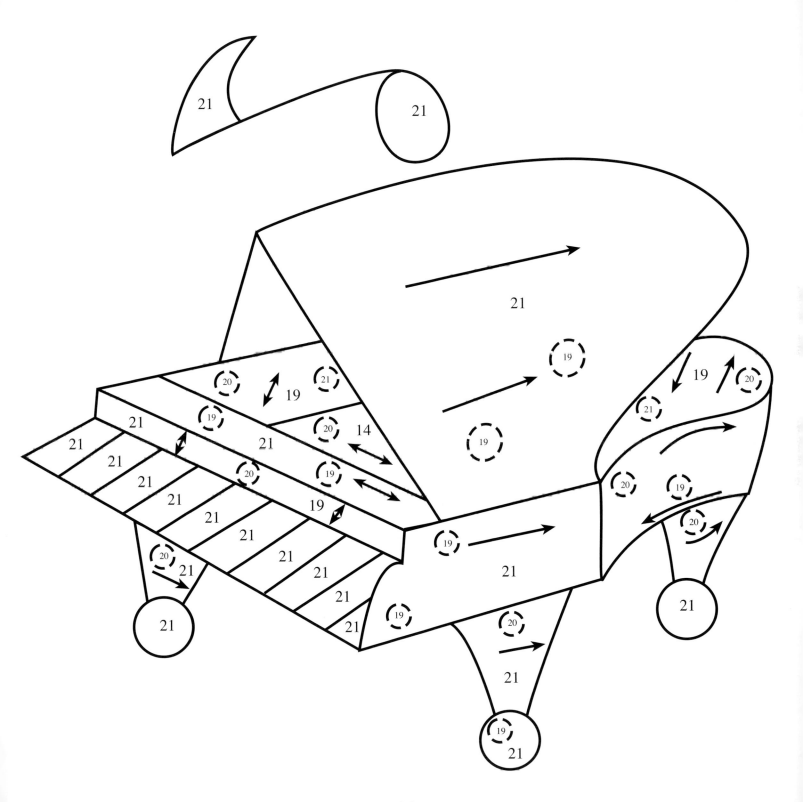

Musical Instruments Pattern/Color Guide

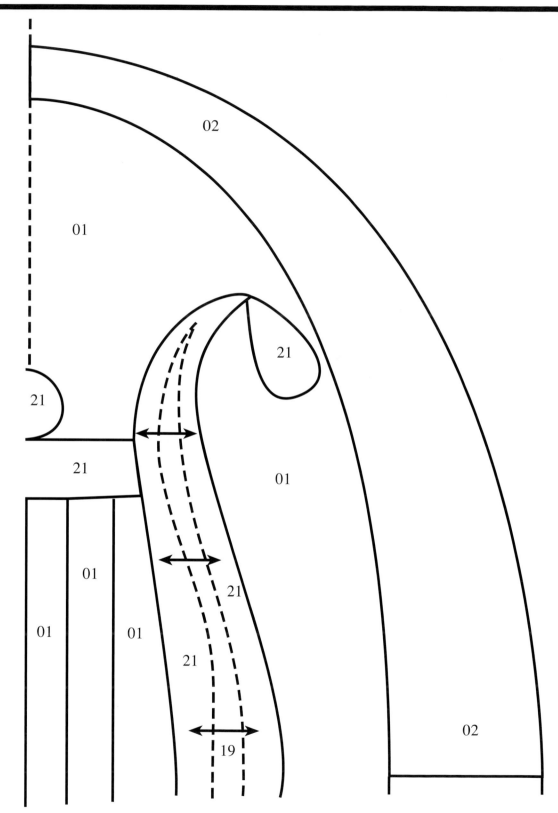

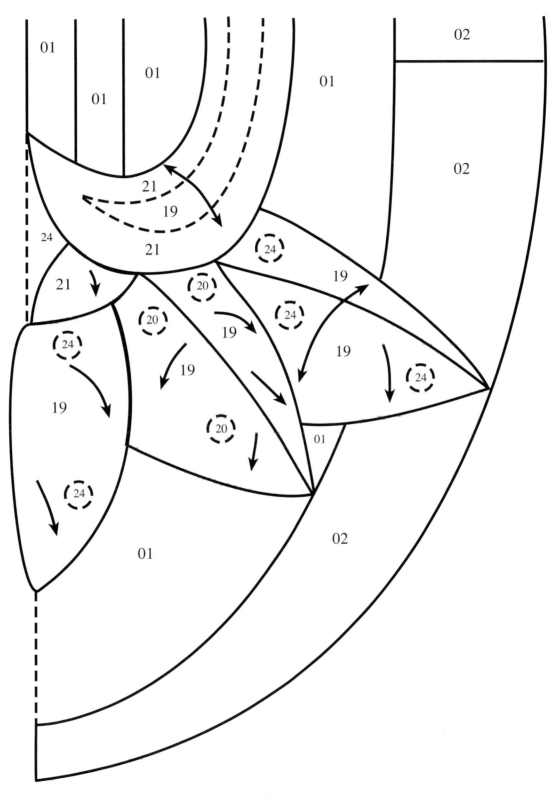

Pond Life

Pictured on page 103

Designed by
Jacque Hennington

GATHER THESE SUPPLIES

Glass Art Paints:
    Amber—20
    Blue Diamond—11
    Cameo Ivory—03
    Cocoa Brown—07
    Crystal Clear—01
    Kelly Green—08
    Slate Blue—13
    Snow White—02
    Sunny Yellow—04
    White Pearl—21

Other Supplies:
    Leading blank
    Liquid leading
    Nutpick
    Premade leading strips
    Ruler
    Stencil brush

INSTRUCTIONS

Prepare Surface:
1. Refer to Window Preparation on page 10. Prepare window surface.

2. Refer to Working with Patterns on page 10. Place Pond Life Patterns on pages 104–107 under leading blank.

Lead:
1. Refer to Using the Modular Technique on pages 15–16. Form pond life motifs on a leading blank with liquid leading. Let dry.

Paint:
1. Refer to Pond Life Color Guides on pages 104–107. Fill in pond life motifs. On some frogs, turtles, and dragonflies, swirl contrasting paints together without blending. On others, dot a contrasting paint on top without mixing. Using nutpick, even paint. Let dry.

2. Transfer Pond Life Border Pattern onto window.

3. Refer to using the Vertical Technique on page 16. Outline border on window with premade leading strips.

4. Using stencil brush, apply Snow White and White Pearl.

5. Apply pond life motifs to window. Connect to corners and create water ripples with premade leading strips.

6. Apply Crystal Clear to background.

7. Fill in water background alternating Crystal Clear, Slate Blue, and Blue Diamond/Kelly Green (swirled together horizontally). Using nutpick, even paints.

8. Fill in remaining background with Crystal Clear. Let dry.

Pond Life Border Pattern/Color Guide

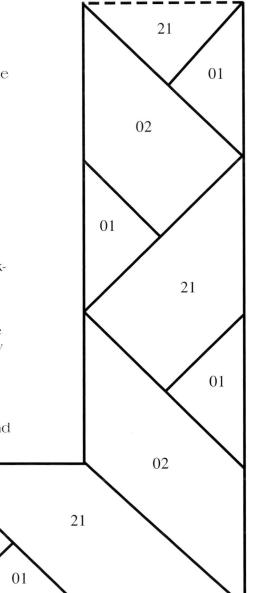

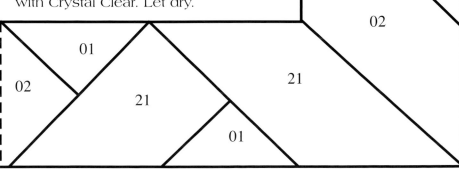

Pond Life

Instructions begin
on page 102

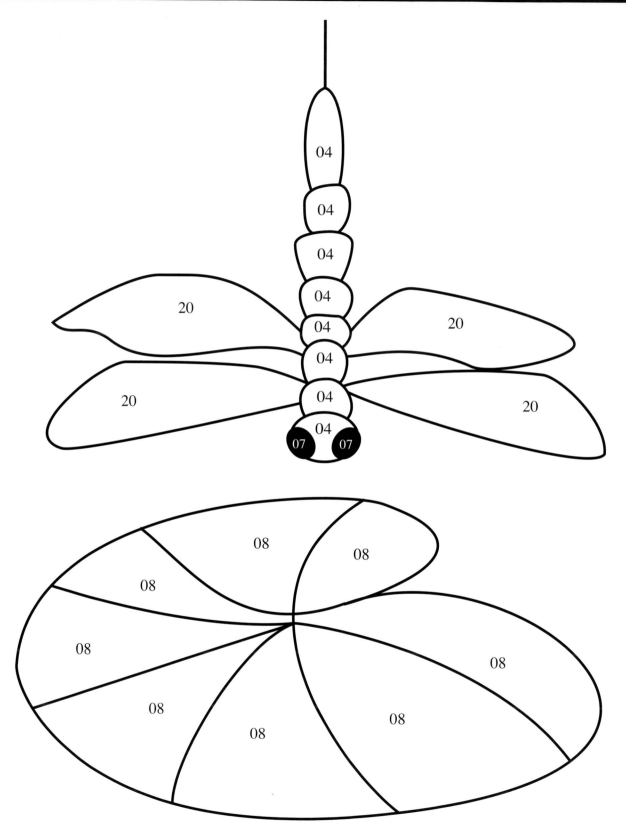

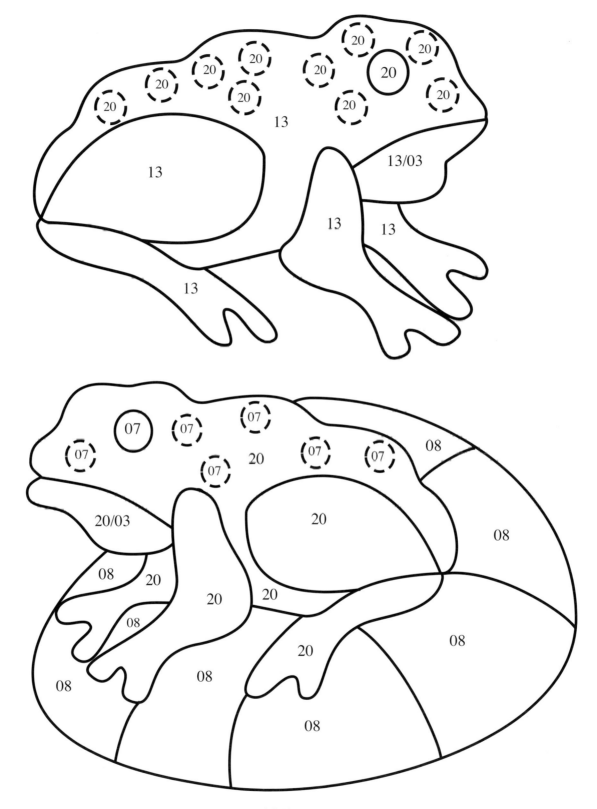

Pond Life Patterns/Color Guide

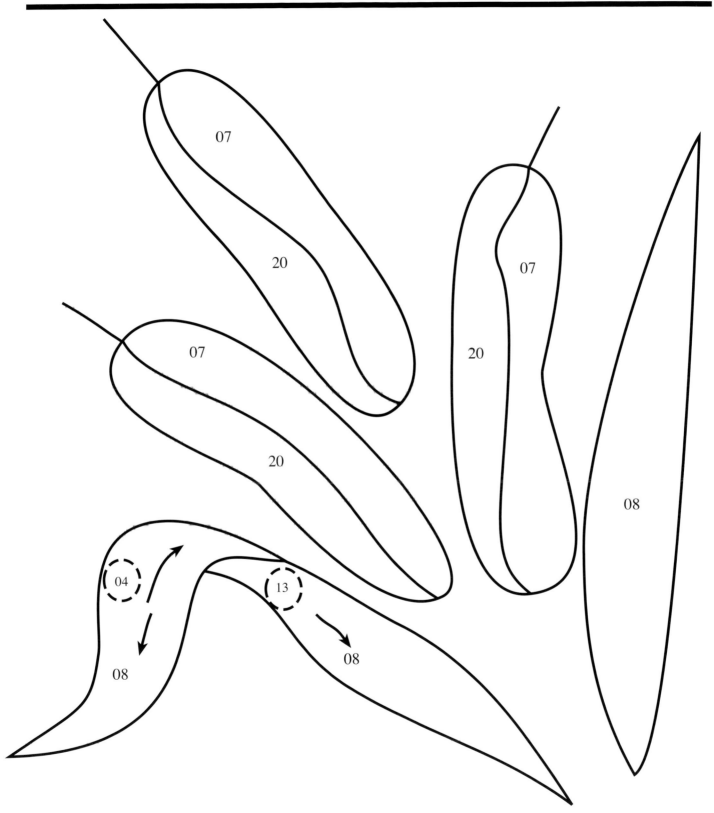

Victorian Tulips

Designed by
Carol Smith

GATHER THESE SUPPLIES

Glass Art Paint:
Crystal Clear—01

Glass Medium:
Etching Medium—44

Other Supplies:
Premade leading strips
Stencil brush

INSTRUCTIONS

Prepare Surface:
1. Refer to Window Preparation on page 10. Prepare window surface.

2. Refer to Working with Patterns on page 10. Transfer Victorian Tulips Patterns on pages 110–111 onto window.

Lead:
1. Refer to Using the Vertical Technique on page 16. Outline tulip motif with premade leading strips.

Paint:
1. Refer to Victorian Tulips Color Guides on pages 110–111. Apply Crystal Clear.

2. Using stencil brush, apply Etching Medium. Let dry.

Victorian Tulips

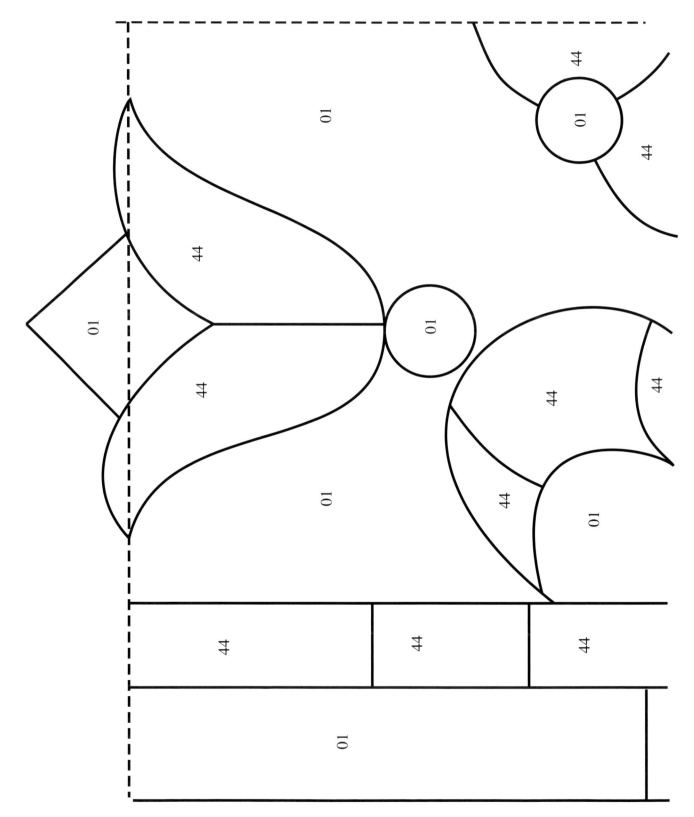

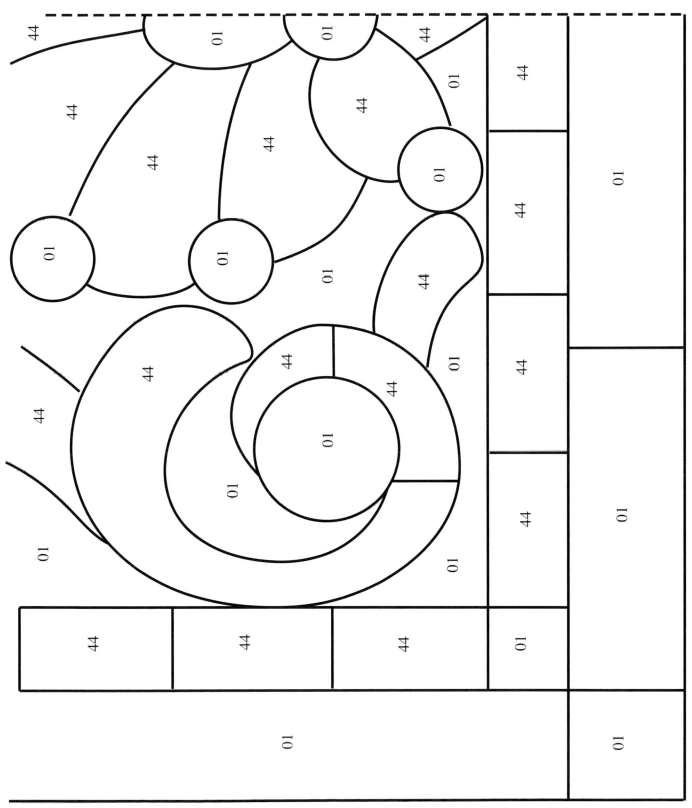

Tulips & Trowel

Pictured on page 113

Designed by
Carol Smith

GATHER THESE SUPPLIES

Glass Art Paints:
 Amber—20
 Amethyst—14
 Cameo Ivory—03
 Canyon Coral—06
 Charcoal Black—18
 Cocoa Brown—07
 Crystal Clear—01
 Gold Sparkle—19
 Kelly Green—08
 Lime Green—35
 Magenta Royale—17
 Rose Quartz —16
 Ruby Red—15
 Snow White—02
 Sunny Yellow—04

Other Supplies:
 Leading blank
 Liquid leading
 Nutpick
 Plexiglas®, desired
  circle size

INSTRUCTIONS

Prepare Surface:
1. Refer to Window Preparation on page 10. Prepare Plexiglas surface.

2. Refer to Working with Patterns on page 10. Place Tulips & Trowel Pattern under Plexiglas.

Lead:
1. Refer to Using the Horizontal Technique on page 14. Outline tulips & trowel motif with liquid leading. Let dry.

Paint:
1. Refer to Tulips & Trowel Color Guide. Fill in design and background. Using nutpick, even paint. Do not comb Crystal Clear. Let dry.

Tulips & Trowel Pattern/Color Guide

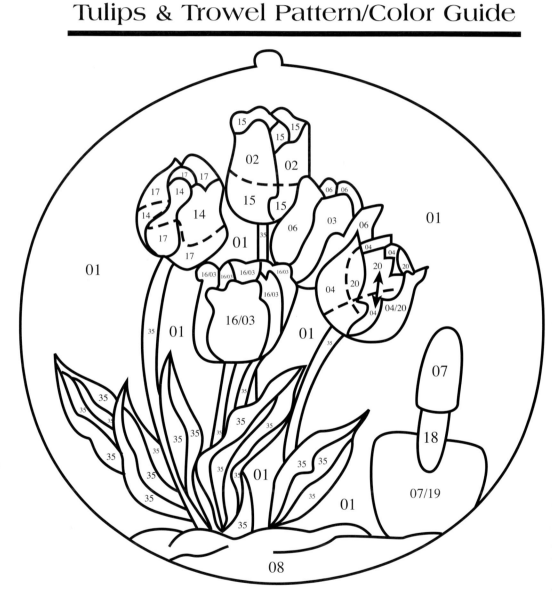

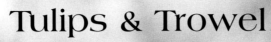

Tulips & Trowel

Instructions begin
on page 112

Birdhouse Screen

Designed by
Julie Schreiner
& Laura Brunson

GATHER THESE SUPPLIES

Glass Art Paints:
   Amber—20
   Berry Red—23
   Cameo Ivory—03
   Cocoa Brown—07
   Denim Blue—10
   Emerald Green—09
   Ivy Green—24
   Kelly Green—08
   Royal Blue—12
   Snow White—02

Other Supplies:
   Hot-glue gun & glue sticks
   Liquid leading
   Nutpick
   Plexiglas®,
      desired rectangle size (3)

INSTRUCTIONS

Prepare Surface:
1. Refer to Window Preparation on page 10. Prepare Plexiglas surface.

2. Refer to Working with Patterns on page 10. Place Birdhouse Screen Patterns on pages 115–117 under Plexiglas.

Lead:
1. Refer to Using the Horizontal Technique on page 14. Outline birdhouse motif with liquid leading. Let dry.

Paint:
1. Refer to Birdhouse Screen Color Guides on pages 115–117. Fill in design and background. Using nutpick, even paint. Let dry.

2. Run a line of liquid leading around perimeter of each panel. Let dry.

3. Hot-glue panels together as desired.

Birdhouse Screen Pattern/Color Guide

Birdhouse Screen Pattern/Color Guide

Mondrian Screen

Designed by
Julie Schreiner &
Laura Brunson

GATHER THESE SUPPLIES

Glass Art Paints:
  Amber—20
  Amethyst—14
  Blue Diamond—11
  Cameo Ivory—03
  Clear Frost—22
  Kelly Green—08
  Magenta Royale—17

Other Supplies:
  Hot-glue gun & glue sticks
  Liquid leading
  Nutpick
  Plexiglas®,
    desired rectangle size (3)

INSTRUCTIONS

Prepare Surface:
1. Refer to Window Preparation on page 10. Prepare Plexiglas surface.

2. Refer to Working with Patterns on page 10. Place Mondrian Screen Patterns on pages 119–121 under Plexiglas.

Lead:
1. Refer to Using the Horizontal Technique on page 14. Outline Mondrian motifs with liquid leading. Let dry.

Paint:
1. Refer to Mondrian Screen Color Guides on pages 119–121. Fill in design and background. Using nutpick, even paint. Let dry.

2. Run a line of liquid leading around perimeter of each panel. Let dry.

3. Hot-glue panels together as desired.

Mondrian Screen Pattern/Color Guide

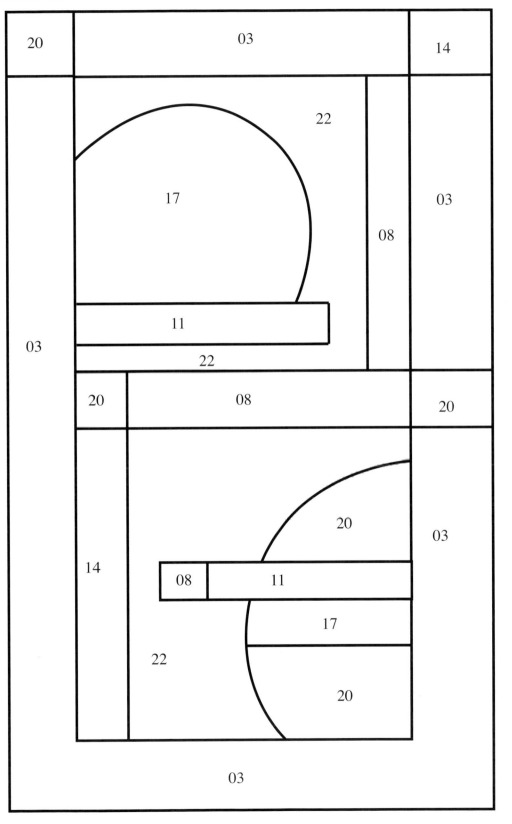

Mondrian Screen Pattern/Color Guide

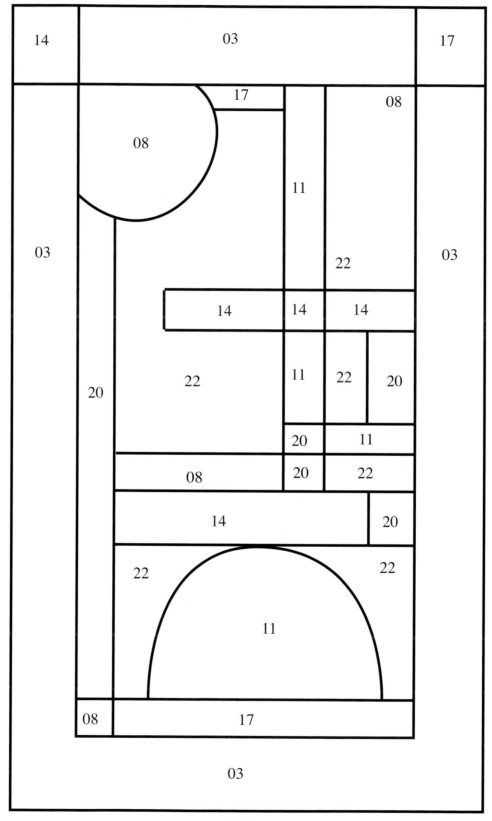

Mondrian Screen Pattern/Color Guide

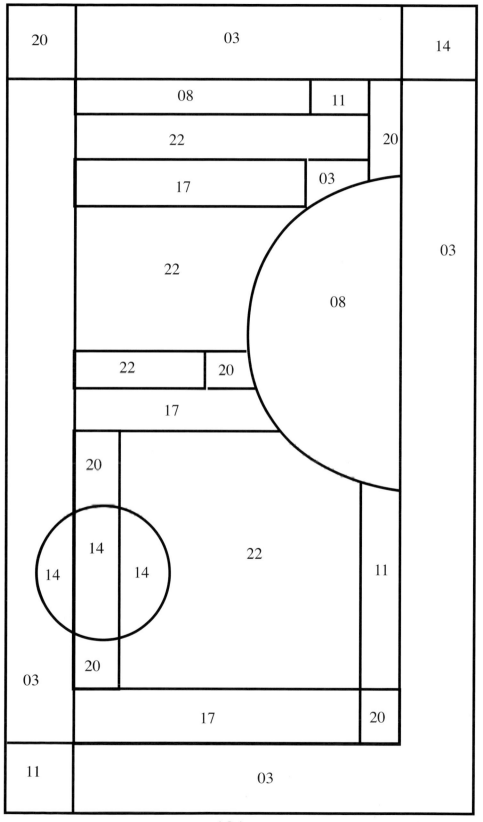

Sunflower Screen

Designed by
Jan Cumber

GATHER THESE SUPPLIES

Glass Art Paints:
Blue Diamond—11
Cocoa Brown—07
Crystal Clear—01
Ivy Green—24
Sunny Yellow—04

Other Supplies:
Hot-glue gun & glue sticks

Liquid leading
Nutpick
Plexiglas®,
desired rectangle size (3)

INSTRUCTIONS

Prepare Surface:
1. Refer to Window Preparation on page 10. Prepare Plexiglas surface.

2. Refer to Working with Patterns on page 10. Place Sunflower Screen Patterns on pages 123–125 under Plexiglas.

Lead:
1. Refer to Using the Horizontal Technique on page 14. Outline sunflower motif with liquid leading. Let dry.

Paint:
1. Refer to Sunflower Screen Color Guides on pages 123–125. Fill in design and background. Using nutpick, even paint. Do not comb Crystal Clear. Let dry.

2. Run a line of liquid leading around perimeter of each panel. Let dry.

3. Hot-glue panels together as desired.

Sunflower Screen Pattern/Color Guide

Sunflower Screen Pattern/Color Guide

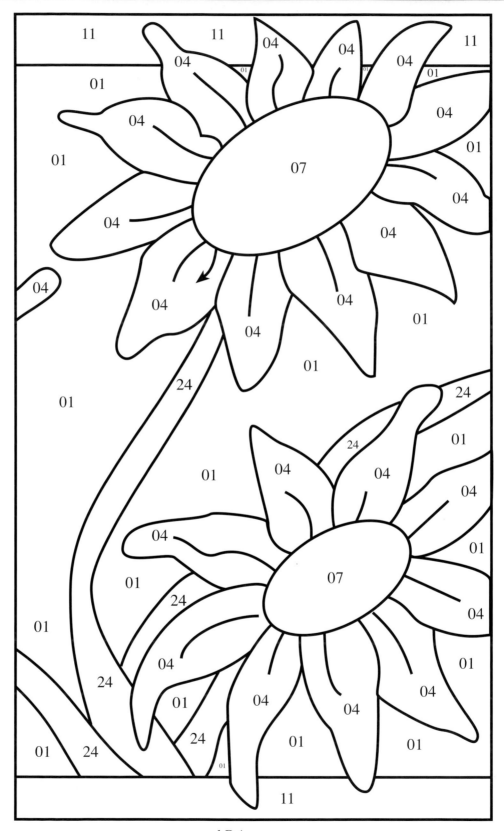

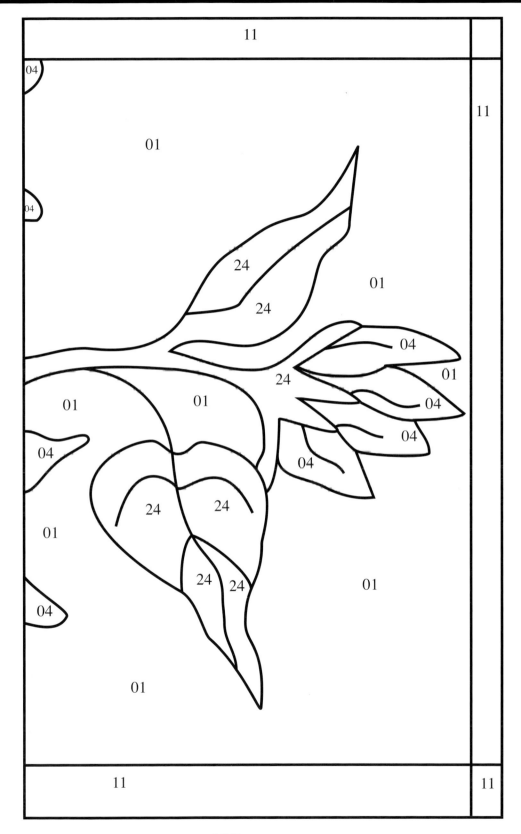

Metric Conversion

MM-Millimetres   CM-Centimetres

INCHES TO MILLIMETRES AND CENTIMETRES

INCHES	MM	CM	INCHES	CM	INCHES	CM
⅛	3	0.3	9	22.9	30	76.2
¼	6	0.6	10	25.4	31	78.7
½	13	1.3	12	30.5	33	83.8
⅝	16	1.6	13	33.0	34	86.4
¾	19	1.9	14	35.6	35	88.9
⅞	22	2.2	15	38.1	36	91.4
1	25	2.5	16	40.6	37	94.0
1¼	32	3.2	17	43.2	38	96.5
1½	38	3.8	18	45.7	39	99.1
1¾	44	4.4	19	48.3	40	101.6
2	51	5.1	20	50.8	41	104.1
2½	64	6.4	21	53.3	42	106.7
3	76	7.6	22	55.9	43	109.2
3½	89	8.9	23	58.4	44	111.8
4	102	10.2	24	61.0	45	114.3
4½	114	11.4	25	63.5	46	116.8
5	127	12.7	26	66.0	47	119.4
6	152	15.2	27	68.6	48	121.9
7	178	17.8	28	71.1	49	124.5
8	203	20.3	29	73.7	50	127.0

YARDS TO METRES

YARDS	METRES	YARDS	METRES	YARDS	METRES	YARDS	METRES	YARDS	METRES
⅛	0.11	2⅛	1.94	4⅛	3.77	6⅛	5.60	8⅛	7.43
¼	0.23	2¼	2.06	4¼	3.89	6¼	5.72	8¼	7.54
⅜	0.34	2⅜	2.17	4⅜	4.00	6⅜	5.83	8⅜	7.66
½	0.46	2½	2.29	4½	4.11	6½	5.94	8½	7.77
⅝	0.57	2⅝	2.40	4⅝	4.23	6⅝	6.06	8⅝	7.89
¾	0.69	2¾	2.51	4¾	4.34	6¾	6.17	8¾	8.00
⅞	0.80	2⅞	2.63	4⅞	4.46	6⅞	6.29	8⅞	8.12
1	0.91	3	2.74	5	4.57	7	6.40	9	8.23
1⅛	1.03	3⅛	2.86	5⅛	4.69	7⅛	6.52	9⅛	8.34
1¼	1.14	3¼	2.97	5¼	4.80	7¼	6.63	9¼	8.46
1⅜	1.26	3⅜	3.09	5⅜	4.91	7⅜	6.74	9⅜	8.57
1½	1.37	3½	3.20	5½	5.03	7½	6.86	9½	8.69
1⅝	1.49	3⅝	3.31	5⅝	5.14	7⅝	6.97	9⅝	8.80
1¾	1.60	3¾	3.43	5¾	5.26	7¾	7.09	9¾	8.92
1⅞	1.71	3⅞	3.54	5⅞	5.37	7⅞	7.20	9⅞	9.03
2	1.83	4	3.66	6	5.49	8	7.32	10	9.14

Product Sources

The products used to create the window projects in this book can be found at most craft and hobby stores. Below is a listing of brand names used for these projects.

Gallery Glass® Window Color™
Transparent Colors:
Amber #16020
Amethyst #16014
Blue Diamond #16011
Clear Frost #16022
Crystal Clear #16001
Kelly Green #16008
Lime Green #16035
Magenta Royale #16017
Ruby Red #16015
Sunny Yellow #16004
Turquoise #16036

Translucent Colors:
Berry Red #16023
Cameo Ivory #16003
Canyon Coral #16006
Champagne #16094
Cocoa Brown #16007
Denim Blue #16010
Gold Sparkle #16019
Ivy Green #16024
Rose Quartz #16016
Slate Blue #16013
Snow White #16002
White Pearl #16021

Gallery Glass® Mediums
Crackle Medium #16049
Etching Medium #16044
Matte Medium #16046

Leading
Gallery Glass® Leading
Blanks #16051
Leading Tip Set #16086
Leading Tips
Micro Leading Tip Set #16245
Liquid Leading®
Black #16025
Gold Metallic #16079
Silver Metallic #16080
Redi-Lead™
Leading Circles #16090
Leading Strips #16089

Brush Set #16224
Includes: etching and feather brushes

Tool Set #16225
Includes: metal combing tool, plastic combing tool, spreader, trimmer

Bevel Molds
Bevel Mold #16781
Contemporary Bevels Mold #16239

Index